FEB. 04
PIE GIRL,
I SAW THIS GIRL ON
T.V. & ENJOYED HER STORY.
THOUGHT YOU MIGHT ENJOY
READING THIS   YOU'RE
WAITING FOR   "
                DAY

pretty good
FOR A *girl*

pretty good
FOR A

THE AUTOBIOGRAPHY

HarperEntertainment
An Imprint of HarperCollins*Publishers*

girl

OF A SNOWBOARDING PIONEER

tina basich

with KATHLEEN GASPERINI

Thank you to all of the photographers I've worked with over the years,
for your patience and encouragement.

Pages 40 and 57 copyright © Bud Fawcett; page 60 copyright © John Bing; pages 64,
77, 82, 89, 119, and 167 copyright © John L. Kelly; pages 70, 138, 148, and 158 copyright
© Scott Sullivan; page 78 (photograph and advertisement) copyright © The Machine;
page 85 copyright © Jon Foster; pages 86, 192, and 208 copyright © Mark Gallup; pages
94, 116, and 135 copyright © Kevin Zacher; page 99 copyright © Tina Basich; page 122
copyright © Lisa Hudson; page 125 copyright © Patty Segovia; page 131 copyright
© Eric Burger; pages 133, 147, 168, and 175 copyright © Justin Hostynek/Absinthe
Films; page 179 copyright © Jeff Curtes; page 202 copyright © Cory Cottrell;
page 226 copyright © Keri Biesinger.

Insert page 1 copyright © Rob Gracie; page 5 copyright © Justin Hostynek/
Absinthe Films; page 7 copyright © Chris Murray; pages 8 and 9 (top) copyright
© Kevin Zacher; page 9 (bottom) copyright © Paul Frank; page 10 copyright
© Jeff Curtes; pages 11 and 14 copyright © Niko Photography.

All other photographs are from the collection of Tina Basich.

FIRST EDITION

Designed by Adrian Leichter

Library of Congress Cataloging-in-Publication Data
has been applied for.

ISBN 0-06-053220-3

03 04 05 06 07 ❖/RRD 10 9 8 7 6 5 4 3 2 1

For my parents, who encouraged me
to discover my own strengths and
follow my heart. And for my brother, who
reminds me to live life to the fullest.

Whatever you can do or dream you can do,
begin it.
Boldness has genius, power and magic in it.
Begin it now.

— GOETHE

Contents

❄ *Concentrating
on the balance
beam, 1977.*

INTRODUCTION

In the 1976 Montreal Olympics, Romanian gymnast Nadia Comaneci achieved five perfect scores of 10. Her performances were the highest achievement in the sport of gymnastics. People all over the world admired her skills. Every little girl wanted to be her. She was on television, on the covers of magazines, and was greatly respected for what she'd achieved as an athlete. No one would have ever said, "You're pretty good ... for a girl." For female snowboarders, it was an entirely different story.

We were the misfits of the misfits—the girlfriends of the rebel skateboarder guys, the anti-cheerleaders. We wanted to fit in, but we didn't. Snowboarding to us was a savior. It was wholly original and something all our own. There were no role models. We made things up as we went along—stickering our boards like our school notebooks, duct-taping our equipment, cutting plastic straps to make bindings smaller around our feet, testing out new tricks. The addiction was instant the first time we figured out how to link turns down a hill. Riding down a natural slope with the wind in your face from the speed you're creating is freedom and that's completely intoxicating.

If we saw another girl with a snowboard on the hill, she was instantly a friend. We knew who she was, maybe not by name, but because of what she was going through. The one thing that connected us, wherever we lived, near snow or not, was our unconditional love for snowboarding. We talked about it constantly and craved the next chance to go ride. It didn't matter if that was every day or once a year. If we snowboarded, we were snowboarders. And therefore, we belonged. In a deep girl niche with our boards as our badges.

When I think back on my life, and how maybe it was unexpected that girls would be so good at snowboarding, I realize that that's what pushed us to take every challenge, pushing through risk, jumping off cliffs, enduring injury, winning gold medals, and managing the fear of death when challenged by Mother Nature. What I don't think people ever knew was that we could do this, that we were made to ride. Our bodies have the grace and rhythm it requires. Our minds have layers of strength and determination. It's instinctual. It took me my lifetime to learn that one of the best places to show this world what women are capable of doing is in the mountains, on a snowboard, riding like the wind.

pretty good FOR A *girl*

Wishing I were
a fairy princess,
age five.

CHAPTER 1

fairyland

I grew up wanting to be like Nadia. I had leotards like hers for my gymnastics classes and learned how to play "Nadia's Theme" on the piano. She was young, brave, and talented. She just rocked it and there was no one like her. I loved gymnastics, too, but unlike Nadia, I always struggled with the pressures to perform. My gymnastics coaches wanted to start training me for the Olympics when I was eight years old because they "saw talent," but I couldn't handle the pressure. I'd get so nervous, I'd pee in my leotard before my floor routine and run off to the bathroom, refusing to come out until my mom came and picked me up from class. What made me quit wasn't the pressure—it was because my coach duct-taped up my hair. I'd forgotten to put it in a bun as instructed, but as my mom said later when she was gently trying to rip the tape off my head, "There is simply *no* need for this." It's ironic that I ended up a professional athlete at all.

Until I was thirteen years old, I lived in a world full of love, magic, and that Christmastime feeling. I was a girl with no preconception of who I was supposed to be or become. I was a tomboy by nature, but unaware of the term. My youth was *Little House on the Prairie* meets *My So-Called Life,* except that even Laura Ingalls didn't spend six months living in a teepee like I did. Although, at the time, I didn't know this was abnormal. We didn't have a TV when we were growing up because my parents sent my brother Michael and me to an alternative school, which did not encourage TVs in the home so that more time could be spent developing creative talents. Thankfully, I was a creative type, or else I'm sure my early years might not have been so pleasant.

We lived in northern California in the suburbs of Sacramento in a little town called Fair Oaks. My parents were high school sweethearts and they married not long after graduation. My mom went to college while my dad took up the trade of house painting. With dreams of a little house on a hill with a white picket fence, they sold their prized possessions— a Jeep and a camera—and managed to save enough money for a down payment on a two-bedroom fixer upper.

In 1969, two years later, I was born. I was two weeks premature and weighed only four pounds, nine ounces, so I had to stay in the hospital for two weeks in an incubator. I was so tiny that my mom would give me a bath with a cotton ball and my grandpa would sing "Tiny Bubbles" every time he saw me. My hair, which was bright red, didn't grow in until I was

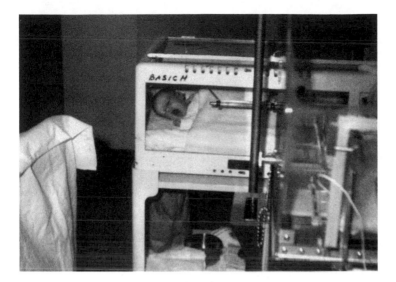

🌸 *Two days old in my incubator, 1969.*

two years old, so my mom Scotch-taped a pink bow to the top of my head so people would know I was a girl.

The first major project on our house was to convert the garage into a bedroom to get ready for my brother, Michael, who arrived three and a half years later. With Michael, our family was complete. We had a dog named Duke, a cat named Princess, a pony named Candy, and five Angora rabbits that we'd card for fur, then spin the fur into yarn on our spinning wheel, and use it for knitting scarves and hats. This was normal to us, although the local paper did a story once and ran a photo with the caption, "What's Wrong with These Children? Hint: Do You See a TV Anywhere Nearby?"

Michael and I lived an imaginative childhood that I only learned later most people cannot believe. We would build go-carts and tree forts all day long and had about ten different tree forts in our yard, with one in almost every tree. We had rope swings and zip lines connecting them like a maze. Michael would always test them, then I'd go down. We'd sit in the plum tree and eat plums and talk about where we were going to hide our next treasure. We'd hide out behind the weeping willow and stare at a dark hole under our deck because a gnome lived in there.

❋ *Reading a story to Michael.*

If it rained, it wouldn't stop us from building something new, and we'd go in to make forts from the living room furniture and the '70s drapes. We'd ride to the 7-Eleven on Candy, tie her up to the ice machine, and buy Popsicles. Or, we'd ride over to Rico's Pizza to play Donkey Kong and my favorite song on the jukebox, "I Love Rock 'n' Roll" by Joan Jett.

My parents didn't let an experience pass us by. They enrolled us in outdoor clubs like Blue Birds and 4-H Club, put us in music lessons, local parades, and ballet classes, took us to summer camp, soccer, softball, gymnastics...we had all sorts of sports and art projects going on all the time. My mom is an artist, and from the beginning she was my biggest inspiration for my own art. She always had a paintbrush in my hand and we would paint together all of the time. I was always painting and coloring. I didn't even know that painting and doing art projects was out of the ordinary until I first went to public school in ninth grade. My new friends thought I was weird when I told them that I sewed my own clothes. Cool, but weird. I thought everyone knew how to sew, or at least paint.

Up until then, we went to a private school called Waldorf. It was an alternative school based around the arts, music, and creative thinking. I claim it's not a hippie school, but we did have gardening, woodworking, and beeswax classes. Our teachers told us endless stories about fairies and gnomes and I really believed in them. My artwork to this day is inspired by those fairy tales, which have even made their way onto my snowboard graphics in a series of Fairy Boards "designed by Tina." I still believe in them.

✳ *Me at the beach, 1971.*

In the Waldorf curriculum we didn't learn to read until the third grade. Instead, we learned about making candles and doing plays and about being creative with our time. I was excited about new art projects and was the kid who couldn't wait to see how my candles turned out. After I finished a project, I was ready to start the next one. We had so many different kinds of classes, like Spanish and German, but also water-color painting, calligraphy, orchestra, choir, as well as the basics—math, science, and geography. Our school required us to take every subject offered, and our whole grade took every class together. Of course, my whole class was only twenty-two kids. Our class assignments were often transferred into our main lesson book, handwritten in calligraphy and accompanied with an illustration or painting.

Waldorf was enchanting. It felt like we were protected from every-thing. We didn't have to think about going through metal detectors to enter the school building or about people skipping classes. Getting in trouble with the teachers was usually over chewing gum or not paying attention. Our class was a small group and there were strong bonds among all of the kids from the things we did together, like walks to the nearby forest where we'd pick wild lettuce and learn which plants were edible. We'd help each other practice lines for the end-of-the-year school play. We even brought in our recorder flutes and would work on making up duets. Everything about the school sparked creativity and our imaginations had no boundaries.

My best friend in fifth grade, Catalin Kaiser, and I created a magic club called TC Magic and Company (the "TC" standing for Tina and Catalin). I created our company identity complete with a rubber stamp of our logo to make stationery on which we would write out spells and magic tricks for our company magic book. Michael would dress up like a clown and be our magical clown assistant. My dad built a trapdoor from my brother's bedroom into the basement of our house so we could have our TC Magic and Company meetings down there and be all mysterious. I so badly

T.C. MAGIC
and Co.

name.   Phone

magic { Tina Basich
        Catalin Kaser
stage { Emily Sullivan
Hands { Jessica Stoffers
clowns { Tierra Primavera
         Timothy McCrany
         Michael Basich

People sell safe food

Dmitri Primavera
or
Dimwetry Primo

wanted to have magical powers and read people's minds that I'd practice thinking deeply about people to see if I could read anything. And I dreamed of being able to fly.

Music was something really important to me and I could hear melodies in my head that I'd write out on sheet music. Writing symphonies and playing all of the instruments was something I dreamed of and my favorite part was naming the symphony and then assigning which of my classmates would play which instruments. When I started any project, I would plan it out to the last detail—symphonies, treasure maps, tree forts, magic companies.

I played the piano, violin, recorder, and the harp. In school plays, I was always the angel because I could play the harp. I played the violin in our school orchestra and was always jealous of Emily Sullivan. She was another good friend and the best violin player in the class and sat in the number one seat of the orchestra. I was seat number two and was always trying to keep up with her. But I got to be the lead singer in the band we later created with Michael. We never successfully played a song—Michael just banged on his drums and I'd make cool sounds on my electric guitar. Emily played the electric violin. Even before our first practice, we had our mom shoot the "cover" photo for our first album.

I was the oldest in my class because I went to first grade twice. The first time around, I went to public school, but on Parents Day, I was sitting there drawing pictures of tulips in different colors and the teacher came up to me and said, "Honey, tulips are red." My mom heard this and picked me up right then and there and took me out of class, and I skipped the rest of the year. I started first grade again at Waldorf the following year.

Being the oldest in my class meant that I got to be St. Lucia on December 13, which is an old Christmas tradition where the oldest girl in the family wears a wreath of candles around her head and brings freshly baked rolls to all the other family members. In this case, we brought rolls to all the other classes. I recently saw Martha Stewart doing a cooking show on how to make St. Lucia rolls. Old traditions are so mainstream these days.

With a great influence from my dad, sports were a big part of my life. My dad was on a softball team and we would always go watch him play and cheer for him. He could hit the ball over the fence and I wanted to be good at sports like him. I'd practice with my dad and brother in the front yard every day after school. The simple fact that I could throw a baseball like a boy gave me so much confidence and recognition around my friends. I was the only girl who'd play flag football with the guys during recess and was always picked for the team first round, which is a big deal when you're a skinny little girl in the fifth grade. They thought I was pretty good and of course I played the part, wearing Dove sports shorts and tube socks up to my knees and carrying my softball mitt to school every day.

Around seventh grade I started to act a little bit more like a girl. My friend Catalin and I went to our first concert, the Go-Go's on their "We Got the Beat" tour. Her aunt was our chaperone and we wore matching outfits with navy blue pleated schoolgirl skirts, white knee-high socks, and sailor tops. I got to wear make up for the first time to the concert and felt so grown-up. I bought a Go-Go's concert t-shirt and wore it to school the next day and thought I was so cool. All the other girls in my class were starting to wear makeup and bras and I wanted to fit in. I asked my mom if I could start shaving my legs like the rest of my girlfriends. She said, "Let's see," and felt my leg. "I don't think you need to yet." I didn't dare tell her that I'd just snuck into the bathroom and shaved my legs with her razor. Being grown-up was going to require different tactics, I decided.

Until I was thirteen, the biggest challenges of my life were simple decisions like whether to take soccer or softball, play the recorder or the violin, paint or draw. Things were familiar and uncomplicated. But in one night, Christmas was suddenly over and the fairy tale ended fast.

*Home sweet
home, 1984.*

CHAPTER 2

another option

I woke up to my mom screaming my name over and over. I ran to the doorway and saw her frantically dragging my brother into the kitchen to get to the phone to call 911. I didn't know what to do or what was happening. My mom was crying and yelling at the 911 operator that Michael wasn't breathing. I thought my brother was dead. He was just lying there. I felt helpless. My heart started beating so fast, but I just stood still, frozen in the doorway, staring at my brother lying on the ground.

While my mom was still on the phone, Michael came to and started breathing again. The paramedics arrived and explained that he had suffered an epileptic seizure. I was thirteen years old; I didn't know what that meant. I didn't know that this would also be the beginning of a long journey for Michael and my family.

Instinctively, I think we knew how to help Michael with his epilepsy, but it was so frustrating. Doctors didn't have all the answers about epilepsy back then and my parents knew that. My mom had to keep searching for what she thought was the best for him and just didn't stop. She was so determined and had stacks of books that she'd read late into the night. If a friend suggested a book that might help, she'd buy it and read it—even if it was about autism, not epilepsy—just in case there might be something in there.

Having a blast with Michael.

When the doctors would give us conflicting solutions, which happened all the time, we'd just keep going with what felt right. The doctors all said my brother would have to be medicated for the rest of his life. My parents would say, "We'll keep looking." But things got even worse.

Michael was put on medication to help with the seizures, and at one point he was taking drugs three times a day. His eyes started to glaze over and he began to withdraw more and more from us and the outside world. It happened gradually, when I look back on it, but he eventually was unable to speak and communicate. It wasn't only the medication making things harder to deal with—there was something else going on.

We didn't know why he couldn't talk and it seemed like he couldn't hear us either, even though my mom had his hearing checked so many times and the results were always normal. I felt like I was losing my brother—my best friend—yet he was right there still living next to me and I wanted to talk to him and play together like we used to. I felt so sad. My mom started writing letters to all sorts of doctors around the country: "My name is Donna Basich and my son has epilepsy and learning difficulties.... He has a difficult time understanding over the telephone, he doesn't seem to have verbal understanding of sounds in relationship to letters, he makes errors copying and presses very hard with his pencil.... It's almost as if he reads lips.... He is intelligent, a hard worker, artistic, and does very well with numbers and shapes.... I hope you can help us and lead us in the right direction."

My parents took Michael out of school because it had become too overwhelming for him and we spent most of our time at home, working on art and woodworking projects with him. The best way for him to speak was making things with his hands. Or he would look at us in a certain way to communicate what he was thinking because we could tell he had an idea or something to say. We had a project going at all times that involved all of us because we wanted to know what he was thinking and that was the only way we knew how. We wanted him to feel confident about himself and thought that would overcome the physical part of his illness. Like mind over matter, only more than that.

But it was so hard to understand what was going on with Michael and it felt like I was going backward, because we used to do so much together and talk and come up with ideas. Now he lived in his own mind. I didn't know how he would be each morning when he woke up—if he would talk

❋ *Playing architect with Michael.*

to me or understand me or not. Sometimes he would have good days where he would say a few sentences and he understood what I was saying, then just as quickly, he'd have hard days and not be able to say a thing and I felt like I lost him again. He would slip into his own world, blocking off all motion and sound, and he seemed like a different person and not like my brother at all. Not the Michael I knew. Each time he would fade into his own world, I kept hoping, Please return the same person.

My mom was always looking for alternative ways to heal, and she followed her intuition rather than listening only to the doctors, no matter what they said. In one of her stacks of books, she came across a description that fit Michael's difficulties—aphasia. It meant inability to communicate and understand verbally. She took Michael to the Scottish Rite Institute for Childhood Aphasia in San Francisco. His test scores said that he was "unable to think and respond to verbally presented material," yet he "demonstrated higher than average intellectual skills in the nonverbal areas." She went to New York on a ticket her mother gave her for her birthday to try to find help at a community in Spring Valley and came home with more books. We tried everything because having Michael on medication for life just wasn't an option. But neither was another suggestion: teaching him sign language. My brother wasn't deaf.

Finally, after seeing a movie called *Sonrise* based on a true story about a boy and his family struggling with his autism, my mom discovered the place that this family founded in Massachusetts, the Option Institute, which specializes in helping families with special needs. She ran out and bought the book on the institute, called, and applied for an appointment.

That same year, 1984, we sold the house that we had grown up in and moved to the property behind it to build a new home. Building a house from the ground up, my mom had read, would be a helpful project for Michael—it would be hands-on and let him work with my grandpa and my dad. Our temporary home was a tepee: my mom had always wanted to live in one because she thought that living in round spaces was healing

❋ *My brother and
I give yet another
performance.*

and good for our family. The whole family was helping Michael with home school, because this was the summer to focus on being there for Michael, helping him communicate and come back to us. We set up camp in our teepee for the summer, complete with a fire pit in the middle, and started construction on our new home.

Our temporary home consisted of a portable toilet, a refrigerator powered by an extension cord from the neighbor's house, and a telephone line coming in from a power line attached to our phone that was mounted in our paint shed. We had a propane stove and battery-operated lamps. For entertainment we had a backgammon game and a trampoline that we jumped on every day that summer. Whether Michael was speaking or not, we always had a blast jumping on the trampoline. I was also trying to do my own things for entertainment; I had an extension cord for my synthesizer, and I would sit for hours and play "Jump" by Van Halen over and over again.

We got plenty of looks from the neighbors. I would hear people in the line at the grocery store talking about us. "Have you seen that family over on New York Avenue living in a teepee?" I wondered if Michael could hear them. I sometimes wished I didn't. Sometimes I really liked living in the teepee because I was so close to my family and I could see that it was helping Michael. But other times, I wanted to just get away. It was pretty tight quarters and, as a teenager, I was definitely ready for my own room with privacy.

I rarely argued with my mom, but one time, I was so frustrated with her about something that seemed so important to me, whatever it was, that I stormed out of the teepee, slamming the burlap door and yelling back, "And for your information, that was me slamming the door!"

It was one of the hottest summers in Sacramento that year, topping out at 100 degrees for days in a row. It was tough living outside, no air-conditioning, no privacy, but I wanted to be there and help Michael and that's what my parents wanted too. I didn't feel like I wasn't getting enough attention and I wasn't jealous or anything, but the three months it was supposed to take to build our house was turning into six months because some of the supplies hadn't arrived on time. I wanted to get back to normal and needed to create my own space. I wanted a flushing toilet and a real shower again. I was so excited about getting my own room eventually that I'd spend time designing the colors of the walls and thinking about different color coordinations with the carpet that I would get. And in the meantime, before we finally moved in, I converted the paint shed into my own domain and moved my synthesizer, a desk for school, and my propane curling iron in there.

Morning to evening

by Tina Basich

In the middle of August, we finally got the call from the Option Institute. On the first ring my mom sprang out of the teepee and raced across the pasture to my paint shed. We'd been waiting for them to call back all summer and felt like this could be the answer to our struggles. We finally got an appointment. But my parents hadn't been able to gather together

Michael and I jumping the summer away on our trampoline, 1984.

the money in time and we couldn't afford to go. It must have been heartbreaking for them—it was for me—but I remember my mom being so strong, not complaining, and turning back to her books and continuing to read. "We have to keep doing the best we can do," was all she said.

A month later, an anonymous friend gave us the money to go to the Option Institute. We could not believe the opportunity and generosity and were so excited. Our ten-day trip there changed our lives. It was confirmation for all of us that our intuition was on the right track. The people at the Option Institute shared with us the importance of living in the moment and learning to appreciate life for what it brings to each of us every day. The idea was to help Michael feel comfortable in *his* surroundings in hopes that he would find his way back to *us*. By living in the moment, and appreciating everything, we could be there for Michael, unconditionally, in a way that would let him know it was OK to be where he was, right then, even if he was confused or frustrated. We had to be completely nonjudgmental and go with whatever was happening, whether he was talking a little bit or completely lost. We would ask him what he was thinking, and if he would talk we'd do big reactions to everything. We'd change our voices often and my mom would try to talk in a rhythmic way—phrases and words that rhymed, because Michael could relate to that and liked musical expressions. I'd try to be there for him in his world, and if Michael wanted to build a fort out of the branches in the backyard, I instantly made that my whole world and would go outside and help him build it.

A few months later back at home, we were playing in my room in the new house and Michael began to talk. He hadn't communicated with words in such long sentences in over a year. We did cartwheels and jumped up and down all over the room. It was one of my happiest moments growing up that I can remember. It felt like my brother was back or at least that he could come back completely. I felt so hopeful and didn't realize how hard it had all been for me, thinking about him so much and wanting him back for myself so badly. But we didn't know how long it would last—we never knew. We took each moment as it came.

It took three years before Michael really started to use his voice again and was able to go back to Waldorf full time. He didn't have to go back because my mom would have home-schooled him if he wanted to, but he chose to go back on his own in the eighth grade. I thought that was very courageous of him—to go back to school and face the challenges of making friends and reading and writing.

The whole experience had quite an impact on me. I couldn't imagine my life without my brother. Instead, Michael became my teacher

Freshman,
sophomore,
junior,
senior.

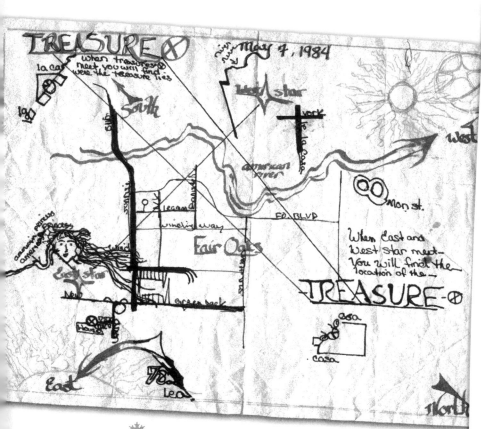

✳ *My treasure map*
of the backyard.

really—I looked at him and took every good moment that came and was appreciative for that moment. He's always reminded me to live life to the fullest because he's true to himself and looks beyond the normal path, creating new ideas and adventures for both of us. That's the kind of brother he is. He taught me the simple mind-set of not needing a reason to be happy and loving unconditionally for the moment that you're in. This would become a thread throughout my life that I would base every important decision on. As a teenager, I was facing different challenges and was often confused about my own life. But forming that bond with my family and my brother gave me an unbelievable appreciation for life, which I think made me into the person that I am.

another option

CHAPTER 3

del campo high

That year my parents and I decided I was going to go to a public high school. I wanted to keep up on my sports and learn more about photography and the public school had more of those things to offer. Plus, I was looking for a more social existence even though I was very shy. I was just curious to see more and know what was out there beyond the white picket fence.

Trying to get ready for my first day of high school, first in the teepee, then in the paint shed with my propane curling iron, was insane. I was so nervous. Up until then, I had only twenty-five kids or less in my class. I wanted to look good and wore my new Esprit outfit. I timidly walked to the bus stop, trying to arrive like a normal kid and hoping no one just saw me step out of a teepee. I was ready to observe my new surroundings, but was only willing to reveal myself in small doses. I didn't want to be too different right off the bat, but I knew that I already had a head start.

Del Campo High School had 1,400 kids. I was overwhelmed to say the least. I made new friends, but didn't fit into any one group and kind of drifted between different cliques. My main niche was with a couple of skateboarders who were the only ones in my school. We'd go by the local skateboard shop, GoSkate, on the way home after school and hang out. I

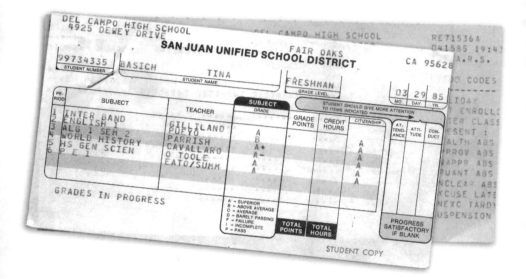

liked the vibe around this shop—it was cool and we could kick back and people did their own thing. I was attracted to the individuality that the skateboard crowd represented. And there was something about those cute skater boys with their hats on backward that got me. I was this new-waver/skater chick who listened to groups like OMD, 7 Seconds, Yaz, and Billy Idol. To this day if I hear 7 Seconds, I recall the smell of that skateboard shop, the grease for ball bearings, and the salty skater guys from sophomore year. I wore tapered jeans with my Vans skate shoes to school with pride and rocked an asymmetrical haircut with a bad perm.

The cool thing about high school was that there were more opportunities to get involved in other sports. I ran track and took swimming and diving. I loved diving because it tapped into my gymnastic skills. However, Del Campo was more competitive than anything I'd ever been used to with so many other classmates and I definitely felt insecure. Even though I was in sports, I was one of many now and found it hard to stand out in the crowd. It was all about being popular, and I didn't fit into the cheerleader mold. I didn't feel like an outcast, just different. Like a tomboy who wanted to be a girl but not too girly-girl, like a pom-pom queen. These kinds of girls were new to me and I felt jealous because they were the popular ones. I used to be popular, but because I played a mean game of tag football or threw a baseball really hard. That didn't matter anymore, and I had no idea how to compete with this new kind of girl. Not that I wanted to compete, but maybe, just a little bit.

I couldn't help being in awe of their perfectly feathered hair and makeup and I wondered how they got their hair so perfect. They must have gotten up so early in the morning. I didn't spend much time getting ready for school because there was no way I could look like them—they were so beautiful and confident. My way to deal with this situation was to wear gold eyeshadow. thinking it went with my hair color. I had lots of friends in high school, but I wasn't considered "popular," which is a big difference.

There was only one guy that I knew of who liked me. He was a new-wave rocker kid and he'd put love letters with lyrics from Depeche Mode in my locker. I would avoid him at all costs, running the other way if necessary, with my heart beating fast. Guys at Del Campo freaked me out, which is probably why I never got asked to any of my school dances. When it came to prom, I knew no one was going to ask me, so I ended up inviting my friend Randy Smith who worked at GoSkate. I had the biggest crush on him because he was a good skateboarder. He bought a new baseball cap and a new pair of Vans for the occasion. I wore a dress that my mom and I had made, which was completely inspired by the movie *Pretty in Pink*. All my friends and I wanted to be fashion designers after seeing that movie. It was so DIY. My mom and I spent days combining four different dress patterns until we got the right look. My prom dress was off-white satin, '80s style, with shoulder pads and a cut-out circle in the back.

On prom night Randy and I got into our rented limo and went straight to the skateboard shop. We cranked 2 Live Crew on the limo stereo and watched my friends skateboard—me sitting there in my prom dress on the curb. I tried to read into every glance from Randy because I had to know once and for all if he liked me or not. I never got kissed on prom night and was disappointed. Maybe my dress was lame. Maybe he was lame. I think we went to the prom for about five minutes to have our pictures taken. Since probably no one would ask me to the senior ball either, I figured I might as well ask Randy to that too, on my prom date. So,

Junior prom photo with Randy, 1987.

a year later we went and did the same thing: took our picture at the ball then went straight to GoSkate to hang out. And again no good-night kiss. I was so over him.

At seventeen years old, I didn't really understand how the whole Dating Thing worked. My first kiss was with Troy Hatler, a surfer boy who I'd met on a trip to Santa Cruz and had kissed only one other time. But for the next year, I didn't kiss anyone else because we'd kissed, which I naively thought meant he was my boyfriend. No one can ever say that I'm not faithful. I'm ridiculously so.

The first official boyfriend I had wasn't the nicest guy. I'm not mentioning any more names, but I made the typical mistake of not knowing any better and thinking that he was going to be perfect for me and be my Happily Ever After guy, so I did everything for him. Even forgetting myself and what it was that I wanted (though I wasn't always sure myself). I always thought of him and tried to think about what *he* was thinking. He was the jealous type, and so I'd lie about going to concerts or movies with friends to avoid confrontations with him when he'd get pissed that I was "having a good time without him." I was too scared to stand up for myself and tell him he was wrong to treat me that way, and ended up in the relationship much longer than I should have been. He ended up breaking it off just when I was going to break up with him, I swear.

Maybe it's from my parents and the fact that they were first loves and things worked out that I think relationships are always the Forever After kind. This wouldn't be the first time I reacted this way. But this first dating experience did lead to my listening to many breakup songs like "Open Your Heart" by Madonna, and massive amounts of energy poured into writing love letters and poems.

Love letters were a big deal in high school among my girlfriends, and my best friend Angie Dominguez and I would sit for hours trying to think of words that rhymed with "heart." Like, "You broke my heart, from the start, but you weren't a part..." We were really bad at poetry, and they were cheesy, but at the time it meant everything to us. I think it was cathartic, too, because after pouring so much energy into these love letters and poems, I somehow felt so much stronger and couldn't believe how long I'd been with such a loser in the first place.

Being the oldest in high school didn't necessarily mean I was the

this dream seemed impossible and
But I was wrong, cause I already kne
found all of this in y
Just a little note to say that
how

I always wondered if I'd ever fare the
in my dreams

In the past tried so hard to
love somone and care,
it was a one sided effort and in the
the end thats just not fair,
the wall of trust kept crumbling,
crumbling to the ground,
inside I'd build it up again and
again it'd just fall down,
the hope for somone true, moved
farther and farther away,
I'd keep to myself and sit and
dream of that special day,
I'd dream of someone that would love
me just for being me,
someone to share my thoughts with, to
show all that I can be,
someone to stand behind me and know
all the right things to say,
someone that knows when to just hold
me until everything's okay

most popular by any means. I got a little more popular only because I was the first to get my driver's license. I did odd jobs helping my dad paint houses, and I managed to save up and buy my first car, a 1971 Volkswagen square-back. My friends and I instantly decorated it with skateboarding stickers. I felt so cool driving it to school my first day of sophomore year. I had a car-pool route every morning to pick up my three best friends, Angie, Heather, and April. The fact that we didn't have to take the bus to school anymore was a huge step into the cool crowd, even though we weren't cheerleaders. We started to get invited to the cool parties on the weekends, maybe because we had a car. It was hard to really know. This car was also the one we used to head up to the hills the first time we went snowboarding.

I loved that car, but a year after I got it, I left it running on our steep driveway with the emergency brake on and ran into the house to get my backpack. I heard a huge crash. My car not only side-swiped my dad's new truck, it also took out the garbage cans and ran into my neighbor's house. It was totaled, I was devastated, and insurance didn't cover it because I wasn't in the car. Like that would have been a *good* thing.

Since I had a driver's license, that also meant I was the designated driver for all the high school parties. My friends started getting into drinking beer on the weekends and since I was always the driver, I never drank. There was definite pressure to drink because it seemed like everyone else did, but for the most part, I didn't want to get into trouble and disappoint my parents. The first time I tried drinking was graduation night, and I got drunk on one beer—or I thought I was drunk—got sick, and threw up in the bathroom.

In high school, I was the kind of kid who was scared to death of speaking in front of the class. It was my worst fear. I'd rather do anything else than get up in front of everyone and give a speech. For my oral report in English, I ended up bringing in my sewing machine to class to demonstrate how to make a pair of surf shorts and, subconsciously, to take eyes off of me and divert attention to the sewing machine. With a nervous, shaky voice, I taught the class step-by-step how to make these drawstring shorts. It ended up being the beginning of a company I started with my friend Mark Horner called Jammers. The next summer we sewed surf trunks on my mom's sewing machine and made up this whole marketing plan, and of course I designed the business logo. We'd go to Santa Cruz and go skimboarding and camping at Brighton Beach Campground, calling them our "business trips" to sell our surf shorts.

Skimboarding in Santa Cruz.

❅ *Boys at the GoSkate curb, 1987.*

When I was sixteen, I discovered snowboarding. Thank God. For me, finding something that I was good at was really important, especially at this age. It gave me something new to focus on and it was exactly what I was made for. Even though I'd been involved in team sports my whole life and learned a lot from them, snowboarding was new and exciting. I loved that. It was completely unpredictable. I really found my confidence through it and so did my brother. It helped him overcome his insecurities of what he was going through with his epilepsy. Snowboarding was our ticket out of that anxious, insecure pit of being teenagers and helped us discover our talents, which we embraced as if our survival depended on it. Snowboarding really became *our* show.

My first day of snowboarding, Soda Springs, California, 1985.

first days

My family was not a snow-family. We lived in the suburbs of Sacramento, so the only connection we had to the mountains was through occasional weekend getaways where we'd build a snowman or go sledding. The two times our family went skiing, we did the typical family ski package thing that included ski rentals, a one-hour lesson, and a sack lunch. We learned to ski and got to the snowplowing stage, which was fun, but it just didn't click. Snowboarding, though, was a lot like skateboarding on snow, which was what my brother and I were all about. Obviously we liked to try new things, and it was the perfect extension of our adventures from childhood. It was uncommon and cool and it sucked us in more for what it represented than for the sport, because at the time it wasn't considered a sport.

I was the only snowboarder at my school, but I got my best friend Heather Mills into it right away. She was the only other girl in my high school who was content with going to GoSkate and watching the boys skateboard on a Friday night. I started to meet all the local pro skaters there and we had the hookup for free stickers and T-shirts. We gave skateboarding a try every once in a while, just to be a part of it, and had our ollies down fairly easily, but that was about as far as our talents in skateboarding went. For some reason, I never felt pressure to get better on my skateboard. In snowboarding, I had such a drive to represent for the girls that I couldn't imagine *not* snowboarding. I guess it was a timing thing. I never saw another girl skateboarding when I was young and didn't realize the significant impression it could make.

I had no intention of being really good at skateboarding. The attraction was to the scene it created. Skateboarders were individuals. I felt like I was a part of something that wasn't really popular, but more like a subculture for the misfit underdogs. At the time it might have just been a difference in a wild hair color, but soon it would mean so much more. By having a skateboard, you were making a statement. But actually skateboarding is very hard to do, and it hurts painfully falling on concrete or wood, which is one reason why I have the utmost respect for skateboarders as athletes.

My friends and I were into the full Sac skate scene. We all had our mandatory skateboards and our Vans tennis shoes. My first deck was a Steve Olson Santa Cruz pro model that I picked out because it was checkered and matched my black and white checkered Vans, like the ones in *Fast Times at Ridgemont High*. I carefully picked out black and red wheels to coordinate with the Independent Built to Grind sticker on my board, and tricked it out with rails and a noseguard. It was so cool I almost didn't want to skateboard on it because it was a showpiece and really quite beautiful.

It didn't matter that we lived in the suburbs of Sacramento rather than downtown with its city skate scene. Most of the time, the best curbs to skate on are at your typical Bank of America, until you get kicked out.

And in the burbs, we found places to build ramps. My dad helped us build one in our backyard. We put skate stickers on everything, including the ramps, and we each had our own tag sign, which we'd graffiti to mark our turf. It wasn't a gang thing, it was more that we were proud of what we were doing, and I'd have to say our tags were pretty creative.

We'd drive to skate contests all over northern California. Skaters like John Lucero, Natas Kaupas, Steve Caballero, and Tony Hawk were the top pros at the time and they were our heroes. I respected these guys for what they could do on a skateboard. The tricks they pulled off seemed untouchable to me.

We had a colorful mix of friends. It was more than just the green-dyed or the red punk rock bracelet and studded belts, the guys had the attitude. I bought into it, standing up for who I was with a "Skateboard ing is not a crime" sticker on my car. While I liked the feeling of being different, I wasn't about to get a Rebel Without a Cause tattoo and thrash about like I hated the world, because I was a skater who liked the world. However, every party or skate contest we went to, there was always the

Heather and I appear in the school paper, the Del Campo Roar, *1986*

Tina Basich and Heather Mills are riding the crest of a hot new sport called snowboarding.

worry and possibility that the guys in our group would end up getting into a fight because we were the punks. Skateboarders love to be skateboarders, and the second some jock, the "real" athlete, cuts them down, telling them they're losers, they're eager to stand up for themselves at any cost. I found myself the getaway driver a couple of times. Like this one time when the guys got into a fight at a house party in downtown Sac. The fight broke out because a jock called us punks, of course, and the living room immediately turned into chaos—furniture overturned, guys throwing punches, guys on the floor wrestling. Then glass started breaking. I didn't know if it was a window or a drinking glass, because in typical fashion, I was already running for the car. Heather was with me and a few of the other skaters hopped in for the fast getaway. The way it worked was that if anyone got separated, we always congregated back at GoSkate. The guys wouldn't get seriously injured because they'd bail before it got too bad. They could deal with getting roughed up and even a broken nose or bruised fist, but the threshold of pain that was never to be crossed was getting too hurt to skateboard. That would just be dumb.

When I first heard about snowboarding, I was attracted to it right away because it was a perfect crossover from skateboarding. My mom came home one day after seeing a snowboard in a ski shop and said, "You guys have to try it, it's like skateboarding on snow." She knew my brother and I would love it.

We rented the one remaining snowboard from the local ski shop in Sacramento and headed up to Soda Springs ski resort. They wouldn't allow us on the chairlifts, so we hiked right alongside the "ski" run. I was wearing my Guess cords, Moon boots, an oversized thrift store sweater, and still rockin' too much gold eyeshadow. The snow conditions were icy, but we didn't care. It was still softer than the concrete we were used to falling on. My brother and I took turns hiking up with the snowboard. We'd strap it on and try to make turns. We fell almost every time and my feet would slip out of my Moon boots and my board would go flying down the hill. I'd be sitting there in the snow in wet cords and my socks. My mom would bring the board back up to me with my Moon boots still stuck in the bindings. We got so many looks from the skiers on the lifts. I knew that they were thinking "What are they doing here?" but like I cared. If anything, I thrived on that attention. Doing something different always intrigued me. I'd lived in a teepee, gone to an art school, and was a skateboard punker. This was nothing.

We had a blast that day. It was nothing like our skiing experiences. There was something special about snowboarding and we fell in love with it right away. It was different from anything we had tried before, but had that same feeling as skateboarding. We were hooked, and my brother and I both bought our first boards the very next day with our Christmas money from our grandpa.

My first snowboard was a Burton Elite 140. I thought it was the greatest thing in the whole world and carried it out of the ski shop with the biggest smile on my face. It was one of the first snowboard designs and had two fins on the tail like a surfboard for turning. It had tall, red highbacks (the plastic bindings behind our heels) on the bindings

❄ *Heather and me at Donner Ski Ranch, 1987.*

that we customized with foam and duct tape for better forward lean and quicker response on our turns. I carefully stickered it up the second I got it home. The first sticker I put on it was "Skateboarding is not a crime." My skateboarder attitude had to be represented, now, as a snowboarder.

By the end of the 1985–86 winter season, we started riding at Donner Ski Ranch in Tahoe because it was the only resort that welcomed snowboarding. Norman Sayler, the manager of Donner Ski Ranch, was so supportive of all of us and just wanted us to have a good time. He saw that this was something new and made kids extremely passionate about getting outdoors and being active. We got season passes for under $150, which allowed us to go up as often as we could all winter. I'd go up with my brother and my friend Heather every weekend, rain or shine. My parents were so supportive and helped out with gas money.

The first time we ran into a few other snowboarders on the hill, we instantly became friends. Back in the day, if you saw someone else with a snowboard, you'd go talk to them and ask about their board, where they got it, what kind of bindings they were using, and when they started. There was always an exchange of advice or tips, like taking out the middle fin from your board to make it easier to maneuver, or using foam inside your Sorrel boots for better ankle support. This was before snowboards had metal edges like skis and snowboard boots didn't even exist. I bought my first Sorrel "snowboarding boots" at the grocery store in Tahoe. I wasn't going to use them for what they were made for, like shoveling snow off the driveway. Our outfits head-to-toe were a mix-match of our Dickies skateboard brand jackets and grocery-store-bought ski glasses. There were no such thing as snowboarding clothes back then. And every time we'd get on a lift with skiers, they'd ask, "What's that?" We'd get so sick of having to explain a snowboard every run and what it was all about that we'd try to ride together so we wouldn't have to answer questions on each lift ride.

Snowboarding was springing up in pockets around the country in

1985, like Tahoe Donner where I started in California and Stratton Mountain in Vermont. Tom Sims, an innovator of skateboarding, was making his mark with his own Sims snowboard brand on the West Coast, while Jake Burton Carpenter, a skier, was heading up the East Coast scene with his Burton snowboards. The seed for these snowboarding pioneers came from Sherman Poppens's "Snurfer," an oversized plastic sled that you stood on sideways like a skateboard, balancing, with a rope attached to the tip. In 1967, when Snurfers were first manufactured, they were considered more of a toy and sold at grocery stores. Like hula hoops and pet rocks, Snurfers faded out.

Skiers considered snowboards a toy, too, like a fad that would probably go away quickly. But snowboarding would prove to be much more than that because we were passionate about what we were doing, although even we couldn't have imagined the impression it would eventually make on sports history.

No matter where we lived, we were a group of people who didn't necessarily consider ourselves athletes, we just liked to snowboard. Snowboarding wasn't even considered a sport. Like the football players who railed on skateboarders because we weren't "real" athletes, snowboarders weren't considered real "snow users" by most resorts and skiers. I don't even think snowboarding was considered a legitimate hobby. We were always misfits—those skateboarders, those graffiti artists. But we didn't care. We were all in it for the love of snowboarding and the adventure that came with it, like making up new tricks and techniques. Snowboarding wasn't something that we did once in a while. If we could, we'd do it all the time. It was a part of our culture—spray painting and stickering up our boards, riding, and tweaking our equipment with files and screwdrivers and duct tape. Lots of duct tape. We'd joke about getting sponsored by duct tape because we used it so much to "customize" our bindings. We'd tape foam to our highbacks to create a more forward angle and duct tape our Sorrel boots all around our ankles for more support. Having duct tape on hand was as important as having a screwdriver, which we needed to constantly retighten the screws of our bindings to our boards. Every snowboarder knew the value of duct tape. In fact, the first-place trophy at the now legendary Mt. Baker Banked Slalom was a gold-plated roll of duct tape. It still is.

Even though we didn't have positive feedback from the everyday crowd at the "ski" resorts (we were always looked down upon as punk kids who got in the way and cut people off, making *their* experience worse), we were going to ride anyway. When I started riding at Boreal, another Tahoe ski resort, you'd have to get a green circle badge or beginner certificate on a card to ride the chairlifts. If you wanted to ride on the more advanced lifts, you had to have an instructor take a run with you and approve that you were capable of snowboarding safely and give you a blue triangle badge. The goal was to work your way up to a black diamond badge, which was the hardest run. Skiers didn't have to take this test to see if they were "safe"—only snowboarders. But most ski resorts didn't allow snowboarding until the mid-'90s. To this day, there are still a few stubborn resorts that remain closed to snowboarders, which is fine with me. Let all the skiers who can't handle us go there.

When Squaw Valley opened to snowboarding in 1988, it was a big deal to all of us because it was like opening up a whole new world. Squaw Valley was new terrain near where we rode, but none of us had ever snowboarded there because it wasn't allowed. We always talked about it because it was so big—it was where the Olympics had been in 1960. At the end of the

❄ *Proudly wearing our GoSkate snowboard team sweatshirt.*

season in '87, Squaw Valley did a trial run and allowed snowboarders to ride on Wednesdays and Thursdays only. Everyone knew about this and showed up to ride the mountain. It was a blast, finding new jumps and secret runs. At the end of the day we ended up taking a big group photo of all of us "outcast" snowboarders in front of the Squaw Valley sign. People were staring at us like, What are those guys doing here? It didn't matter though because we were there to stay.

Squaw opened to snowboarding full time the next season.

Our little group of snowboarders was growing. We now had people to look up to who inspired us to become better snowboarders. Guys like Damian Sanders, Chris Roach, Terry Kidwell, and Shaun Palmer were pushing the sport with new tricks and smooth style and defining a new freestyle snowboard movement. Their tricks were directly influenced by skateboarding, even carrying the same names, like Method Airs, Indy Airs, and Handplants. Damian taught me how to do his new trick, a cross rocket, a version of a Rocket Air with your hands crossed over, grabbing the top of your board. I guess not many people can say they learned how to do a cross rocket from the legendary Damian Sanders. He was always trying something new. Different variations of skateboard moves were in the works at all times and new standards were being set.

I always felt the support from the guys and included in their scene. They were impressed that I was out there trying to learn the tricks and keeping up with them on the mountain. In skateboarding, the only impressive thing I could do was an ollie on a curb, which everyone, including myself, considered pretty good for a girl. In snowboarding, I was much better—even keeping up with the guys. It was the perfect sport for me and it was something that I was good at and made me stand out from others at school. It gave me confidence. The first publication to run a picture and story about me snowboarding was my high school paper, the *Del Campo Roar*. I was getting recognized for doing this cool new sport. I was the snowboarder girl.

First day of snowboarding at Squaw Valley, California, 1987.

how to be prepared for your first day of snowboarding

❈ **Your equipment makes or breaks** your experience on your first day of snowboarding. Snowboard boots are so important! There's nothing worse than having your feet hurt on your first day from uncomfortable boots. Working in a new pair of boots can be brutal, so it's worth it to walk around in your snowboard boots in your house before you go riding. I have tried everything from running them over with a car to make the pliable plastic and stiff foam more flexible, to soaking them (if they're leather) in the bathtub and then wearing them until they're dry. In the end this wasn't the best solution.

Make sure you have some sort of waterproof clothing, especially pants. You will spend most of your time on your butt your first day. That's just the learning process. It's OK to wear your old ski gear. It's way better than wearing wet Levi's all day long. Whatever it takes to keep you dry, wear it. Thrift store snow outfits work great, too, so go for the vintage look! It's better to keep warm than think you're cool with only jeans on and a light jacket. I overdress all the time with many layers. It's easy to shed a layer if it's too warm out, but harder to keep warm if you're not dressed properly.

Gloves or mittens are a must. I find getting in and out

of your bindings is a little bit easier with gloves, but some people prefer mittens for warmth. Sometimes ice can build up in your bindings and you need your fingers to scrape it out. I recommend goggles over sunglasses, unless you're just "plaza surfing" (hanging out at the lodge). Glasses fall off your head more easily when you fall, and the wind in your eyes can get bad at high speeds. I always wear a hat and goggles in any condition. If it's a snowy day I bring a neck gator. This keeps snow from falling down inside of your coat and keeps your neck warm. These are sold at any ski or snowboard shop and are worth the $10 to save your chin from chafing on your jacket zipper, too.

Sunscreen is a must and always needed. There's a double glare from the sun on the snow, and with the altitude there's a much higher level of sun exposure. Even with sunscreen on every day, I still get new freckles from those sun-blasting days. I always try to reapply throughout the day if I'm hiking and sweating. Don't forget your ears and neck, and if you're sporting braids and no hat, it might be a good idea to sunscreen your part. I know it sounds gross, but a burned, peeling scalp is much worse. I use Clinique Body SPF 25. It seems to stay on and isn't that greasy.

And last but not least, do a fifteen-minute stretch before heading to the hill. This helps to prevent injury and sore legs and a sore neck the next day. I even do leg stretches throughout the day in the lift lines if my legs start to cramp up.

I always listen to music on my way up to the

mountain. I love having a song stuck in my head for the day (as long as it's a good one). My favorites are anything from old Madonna to Metallica, depending on what kind of mood I'm in. I'm not a fan of riding to music with earphones. It's a blast riding to music, but it's so unsafe to not hear what's going on around you. One time, I was up at Mt. Hood in Oregon during the summer, cruising down the hill with my headphones on and clueless to my surroundings. I saw some friends on the lift waving to me so I started to slow down to see what they wanted and just as I stopped to take my headphones off, a 100-pound bag of salt went flying past me going about 60 miles an hour. It missed hitting me by about a foot. It freaked me out and I never rode with headphones again—that bag could have broken both of my legs. For those of you asking, What's a 100-pound bag of salt doing flying down the hill? Well, the ski resorts use salt to harden the snow. At Mt. Hood on the glacier in the summer, they sprinkle salt on the runs and halfpipe to keep it from getting too slushy. The bag had fallen off a snowcat that was hauling it over the halfpipe.

It's really important to have a good breakfast before you go snowboarding. It will get you through the day, and if the snow's good, you won't want to stop. I always bring a PowerBar in my pocket just in case I decide to skip lunch for powder turns! ✳

how do I choose a snowboard?

❋ **The snowboard you choose is an**
important decision. Ask yourself two questions: (1) What
level snowboarder am I? (Beginner to expert) and
(2) What type of riding am I going to be using the board
for? (snowpark, halfpipe, freeriding, big-mountain riding).
It's best to get your board from a snowboard shop, not
out of the newspaper or at a garage sale (unless you
already know what to look for).

Normally, a snowboard standing on end next to you
should come up to between your chin and the top of your
head. The longer boards are better for deep powder and
hauling ass down a big mountain. Shorter boards are best
for halfpipes and park jumps and generally for freestyle-
type riding. When you go to a shop definitely ask for help.
Tell them what level you are and what type of riding you
are planning on doing. Even tell them what ski resort you
ride at, because this sometimes can help them figure out
the right board for you.

Boards range from the plastic ones at Toys "R" Us
for $100 to $600 for a real board. There are a lot of brands
to choose from. Your weight will determine the stiffness
of the board. The heavier you are, the stiffer the board.
You want the board to hold your weight in a turn and not
wash out like a noodle. Also the tip and tail shape are
important. A longer tip is generally for freeriding and

a shorter blunt tip shape is for halfpipe and park. The tail of the board is important as well. It should have a similar kick up from the ground. Only race boards have a flat tail like a ski to gain more edge contact. It's great to rent a few boards first (if you can afford it) to get the feeling of different types of boards. Some resorts have snowboard demos where the different companies loan out boards for the day. This is a great way to test the product before you purchase.

I bought my first board at a ski shop in Sacramento for $149.99. There was only one kind at the time, the Burton Elite 140, and they only had two of them. My brother and I each bought one. I sold mine for $100 a year later to upgrade to my Sims Pocketknife. Five years later I came across the guy who bought it on the hill and I bought it back from him for $250 as a keepsake. ✱

how do I choose my stance?

✱ **If you already participate in** skateboarding, surfing, or wakeboarding, you would most likely continue to use the same stance on a snowboard. Otherwise, try standing with both feet straight on the ground and have a friend push you from behind. The foot you step forward with is usually the foot you put forward on your snowboard. In high school when I started snowboarding, I naturally just put my right foot forward, which means I ride "goofy foot." Right foot forward is called "goofy." Left foot forward is called "regular." The most common stance is a 0- to 3-degree angle on your back foot, angled toward the front of the board, and a 15- to 18-degree angle on your front foot toward the front on your binding setup. Stance widths vary according to the size of the snowboarder. A good solid stance is shoulder distance apart. I ride about a 19.5-inch stance. I'm about 5'6" and weigh 115 pounds. If you put your stance too wide (big stance), you have less control of your snowboard and you look like a dork. In the early '90s the "big stance, fat pants" fad was the trend. It was fashion, not function, but everyone was trying it.

I think my biggest stance was around 21 inches between my front foot and my back foot at the most. Every once in a while I'll see a beginner on the hill with an old or borrowed snowboard with a 27-inch stance. Nothing but straight legs and no edge control and they're barely getting down the hill. If you see someone struggling, stop and give them a quick tip to go into the snowboard rental shop and have them fix their stance. You have all odds against you with the wrong equipment and setup.

When you first mount up your board, put your boots on and strap into your bindings to get the feel of the stance and make sure it feels comfortable. On the living room carpet always works best for me. The top of the mountain is the last place you want to be when you realize your stance is all wrong.

Another tip: Every time you head for the hill, it's important to check your bindings and make sure they're on good and tight. I've been up at the top of an untracked powder run with a loose binding and it sucks to have to walk back to the top of the lift to tighten it up while someone else takes your powder line. It's too risky to ride with a loose binding. If it ripped off the board in a turn, you could get really hurt. I always try to pack a compact screwdriver in case I have a screw loose (ha ha). These days you can get these mini screwdrivers that tuck into your coat or pack without the tip sticking out. A lot of rental shops carry little portable screwdrivers for snowboard bindings. ❄

❄ *Charcoal drawing from high school art class, 1988.*

At seventeen, all I needed was my VW and my snowboard.

snowboarder girl

As far as being a pioneer in snowboarding, it was completely by default. I didn't know that what I was doing would have an impact on other women, and that girls coming into the sport were watching what I was doing on the competition circuit. Professional snowboarding had never even existed before and I was not a rockstar aside from being in the *Del Campo Roar*. And that quickly faded because most people didn't see what I did, and it wasn't like I'd go to school on Mondays and announce the latest competition I'd placed in. I think one of the main reasons why snowboarding is so different from other sports in terms of pro athletes is because we never had any hang-ups or ideas of what things were supposed to be like. We all started from nothing, so we had nothing to lose. We shared ideas to get better because we were all in it to make the sport better. So in competitions, we were supportive at the top of the starting gate. Everyone knew what the other person was trying to accomplish and we'd be excited for one another when one of us landed a new trick because that meant the bar was raised. Unlike most competitive athletes, after the competition we often rode together for some last runs of the day. This sort of camaraderie was especially true among the women snowboarders, and it was so important because there weren't many of us out there. We had to be there for each other and to represent.

When I first started snowboarding, I caught on pretty quickly by following the group of snowboarding guys around. Most of the time I was just trying to keep up, but in time I was setting my own pace and attempting all the tricks and jumps that the guys were doing. The guys would say, "You're pretty good, for a girl," and I would always respond, "Thanks!" It was a compliment to me. I did feel pretty good. On the other hand, they never said that to me in gymnastics. The "for a girl" part made me wonder if I was really accepted or one step out of their guy club. In the beginning I was so excited to hear that, because up until that point, I really didn't need to hear more. I had never gotten more than that in skateboarding. The difference was I was a much better snowboarder than I ever was a skateboarder. I was in it from the start like they were. I went for it, too, doing new tricks, trying harder to get better. Snowboarder guys weren't going to discourage me, because I was already trying harder than most of the guys out there. Slowly, it started to confuse me when I heard that expression. Like, "Yeah? What if I was just 'pretty good'?" But maybe that would be too close to admitting I was as good as they were.

At my very first snowboard contest at Donner Ski Ranch, there wasn't even a question of whether or not we were going to enter. If you snowboarded, you were obligated to be there. Everybody in the Tahoe scene who snowboarded competed. At the time, I knew how to turn on my board but had not tried to catch air yet. I was still working on linking my turns and stopping at the bottom of the hill without falling.

Still, I entered. There were two disciplines, halfpipe and slalom. The halfpipe was really small compared to the Superpipes of today, which are now built with specialized Pipe Dragon snow machines and are 12 feet deep. Our first halfpipes were made simply, with snow that we pushed up the sides shoveled by hand, forming our closest version to a skateboard ramp.

There were four girls entered in the Women's Open division—the only division there was for women. I wasn't nervous at all, even though this was my first contest. The simple fact that I was a snowboarder gave me confidence. I was doing something with my peers. It was a different feeling than competing in gymnastics. The pressure didn't exist in snowboarding yet. There were no coaches telling me what to do, how to warm up, what my routine should be, or what score I had to get. This was one of the very first snowboarding contests ever. The judges were the people who worked at the resort, and they didn't know what to do either. This was the beginning.

Most of us went down the halfpipe and just slashed the sides without getting air, but Bonnie Learey, one of the few other women snowboarders, impressed everyone by adding an ally-oop slide. Unfortunately, on my second run, I had taken the advice of Mike Jacoby (who would later go on to become a champion World Cup snowboard racer), who told me if I hit the jump that was at the very end of the pipe and caught air, I'd win. Well, I'd never successfully gone off a jump before, but the thought of a first-place trophy sent me down the pipe heading for that jump. I hit it, flew through the air, and landed flat on my back. I couldn't move. My mom and dad rushed over with the ski patrol and I ended up taking an ambulance to the hospital to get my back

❇ *GoSkate sticker that
ended up on
everything I owned.*

checked out. I had muscle spasms, but nothing too serious. Looking back on it now, I realize that if I had been seriously injured that would have been the end of the beginning for me. But at the time, all I could think about was my third-place trophy, my first snowboarding accomplishment. I was so proud.

In the late '80s the formats for competition changed and included moguls, halfpipe, giant slalom, and dual slalom—where you'd race around

❋ *My first contest, Donner Ski Ranch, 1986.*

what were called "gates," or poles in the snow—similar to ski racing. I continued to compete in local contests and started to get my share of first-place finishes. Eventually there were enough girls entering contests to divide into amateur and professional divisions. That's when I turned pro: I just checked the pro box on the entry form one day and that was it.

I was getting a lot of attention at these local contests for my aggressive riding and the few tricks I could do, like my tailgrab and ally-oop slide, and my consistent contest results. I had the support of GoSkate, who would pay my entry fees, and received my first free snowboard from Sims. Hippo clothing out of Sacramento hooked me up with a new snowboarding outfit, which replaced the windbreaker my brother and I had silkscreened with "Sac Pac" across the entire back. There's nothing better than getting free stuff when you're seventeen years old.

My parents would come to as many contests as possible and watch us. They weren't really snowboarders or skiers, but often they would help out with the contest as gatekeepers and starters at the starting gate. At the end of the final California Series contest at Soda Springs, we had a Chinese Downhill competition for all the parents to see who could get down the hill fastest on their kids' snowboards. My dad came in second to Tucker Fransen's dad and my mom won it in the moms division. My parents were very supportive of my snowboarding because they could see how much I loved it. They also liked the fact that my brother and I were doing this together.

We would do anything we had to in order to get on the mountain and go snowboard. We could always rally a group of riders to carpool up to the mountain. We would use paper clips to attach our lift tickets so that we could drop them from the lift to our friends waiting below. They'd catch them and use the same lift tickets to get up the hill so everyone would make it to the halfpipe to practice. If a competition was out of town, we could fit at least seven to ten people in one hotel room. Driving up to the mountain, I always had an eager feeling in my stomach and couldn't get to the halfpipe soon enough. I'd have my winter socks already on, most of my clothes and my boots ready to lace up so I wouldn't waste any time in the parking lot. I didn't want to miss a thing. Anything could happen. Someone could be pulling off a completely new trick.

By 1987, I was good enough to enter the newly formed World Championships in Breckenridge, Colorado. I was seventeen and this was my first trip away from home. I was so nervous. Heather traveled with me. This was bigtime—an out-of-state snowboarding competition. My parents bought my ticket and I had a little bit of money saved up from birthdays and side

Waiting for the results to come in.

jobs that I used for spending money and for food. We had some connections with other snowboarders from Tahoe who were going out for the contest, so we had floor space for lodging. GoSkate paid my entry fee as part of their "sponsorship" for me as their shop athlete at a world championship, so I wore their GoSkate T-shirt to represent.

I'd been riding and training hard for this contest, sometimes even skipping school Fridays to go ride. As long as I kept up with my grades and my homework, my parents were cool with me taking an extra day to ride, especially when I told them I was practicing for a world championship. But it was really different than what other kids in school were doing, like going to basketball games and having the school bus take the team to their game, then home afterward. There wasn't a busload of snowboarders coming with me, singing rallies, or taking me home that night if I lost the game. It was just Heather.

This was my first big contest to test my own skills against other professional women who were mostly teenagers like I was. Girls like Susie Riggins, Jean Higgins, Kelly Jo Legas, and Amy Howitt were part of the lineup, and none of us knew what to expect.

When we arrived, we immediately went to the resort to sign in and get our competition bibs, then check out the pipe. I looked around the lodge at all of the snowboarders signing up. There were so many of us. Up until this point, it seemed like our little Tahoe scene was all that existed, but it was so much bigger now. It's a different feeling knowing that there are other snowboarder girls "out there somewhere" versus actually being with them, checking in to get your competition bibs so you can compete against them.

❄ *Early days at the California*
Series contest with the girls.

Plus, the halfpipe seemed huge. It was so much bigger than the one I was used to at Donner Ski Ranch that I fell during practice just trying to drop into it. This did not help with my already shaky confidence. My stomach had that nervous feeling like before a gymnastics meet. All of the other girls were ripping, it seemed, and I felt like I wasn't snowboarding my best at all. Amy Howitt was doing airs an entire foot out of the pipe, and until this point, I'd never been truly impressed by another girl snowboarder. I wanted to do airs like she did on my snowboard. Some of the other girls had new tricks and I checked them out and tried to remember them so I could practice their moves when I got home. In my competition run, I did a two-handed backside method and a frontside indy air, which was all I had in my bag of tricks, so I just repeated them all the way down the pipe. There was no way I could try my ally-oop in a pipe this big. But I ended up placing sixth in the halfpipe, and thought, "Does this mean I'm sixth in the world?" Possibly.

I was so excited!

During the same contest, the guys were pushing the levels of the sport with huge airs out of the pipe. Craig Kelly was the favorite in the guys division with his smooth frontside slob airs. Shaun Palmer was catching the most air with big backside rocket airs about five feet out of the pipe. They were superhuman to me. I couldn't imagine that girls would reach that level of riding. Still, we were definitely pushing it in our own right and we had a good showing for the women's division.

Toward the end of our trip, Heather and I were approached by a film director to snowboard in a commercial for Wrigley's spearmint gum. I called home and told my mom that some guy from Hollywood wanted to put us on TV and he would pay for our hotel if we could stay with him for another two days. I'm sure it sounded fishy the way I blurted it all out, and she told me it "probably wasn't a good idea" and that "it was time to come home."

Even without the commercial to our credit, we were all starting to

SNOWBOARDING!

The latest trend on the slopes this year is snowboarding. Young surfers and skateboarders have found a winter pastime that is growing rapidly in popularity.

Most snowboarders are males between the ages of 15 and 25,

Tina Basich photographed by Bud Fawcett, courtesy of Boreal.

get sponsored with snowboards, boots, and clothing, and things were changing fast. We were surprised by all of the attention we were getting. Luckily, as snowboarders, the group of people who started in this sport were so creative and aggressive but not necessarily the kind of people who looked for attention. Like other snowboarders, I'd go back to school and most people didn't know where I'd been or care that I'd just placed sixth in the world. The big news on Monday was that Del Campo had won the football game.

Sometimes after riding so hard in the halfpipe all weekend, I could feel the pain and stiffness set in. It wasn't unusual on Monday mornings to wake up for school and not be able to lift my head up off the pillow because of whiplash from the latest crash. It would take so much effort to lean forward, put my feet on the ground, and make my way to the shower. I don't think cheerleaders ever felt this way. I doubt they went to the chiropractor later in life as much as I did either. Once I turned pro and could afford it, my chiropractor became a new friend, putting my back in line every other month. He would compare the extent of my condition to that of car crash victims because often I was worse off than his car

✳ *At the World Championships in Breckenridge, Colorado, 1987.*

patients. He'd say, "Well, Tina, don't worry, this time it's only a small car crash—a Beetle alignment." The Ford truck crashes practically took me out completely.

Even with a bad case of whiplash or stiff leg muscles and bruised shins, I got ready every morning because I really liked public school and wanted to do well. At Waldorf, they didn't have a grading system; the teacher would give us feedback and comments at the end of each month on a one-on-one basis about the quality and artwork and completed answers in our lesson books. In public school, I was graded A through F, which was new to me. And I have to say, I liked it. It was competitive and

I could see exactly where I stood. I was almost a straight-A student, but teachers thought I did weird things. In public school, my assignments would be on Xeroxed copies, plain, black and white. No calligraphy, no expectations of applied color, we just had to do the assignment. So, for example, in biology, I would color in the black-and-white Xeroxed frogs that we had to describe on our assignment paper. I'd shade in the frog's skin in various shades of green, lighten the underbelly, make the heart a deep-red rose with layers and layers to show potential palpitation. I don't know why I would do this. It just seemed like I should because the frog was blank and boring. Sometimes the teachers would hold it up in front of the class and say, "Look at the extra effort Tina put into her assignment. Not exactly what we were thinking of for extra credit, but..." My classmates would look at me and were like, "Why did you color in the frog?"

Nobody thought I was weird in snowboarding. We were all different and making up our existence as we went along. For women snowboarders, we were not only the weird new athletes, but *girls*, so we needed to push each other in a supportive and positive way for our sport to grow, but more important, so that we could all feel like we belonged. It would have been crazy not to support the other girls. Some of these women, like Barrett Christy, Shannon Dunn, Morgan Lafonte, Michele Taggart, Bonnie Zellers, Amy Howitt, and Jean Higgins, made their marks in the sport, and they were always pushing the limits of what people thought women could do. They were even better than most of my homeboys at Donner. I looked up to them and they gave me the inspiration to push myself to new levels and go beyond what most people thought possible. By being together, and competing and being supportive of each other and excited about what we were doing, we didn't fade out, and instead paved the way during those early contests to make a permanent place for women in snowboarding competition.

To keep up with our demands and improved riding abilities, snowboarding equipment was also changing rapidly. Duct tape was less neces-

Dropping In

❄ *First published photo in a snowboard magazine, I.S.M., 1988.*

Photo: John Bing

Snowboarder: Tina Basich

ISSUE 5

I don't have to tell you that the focus of this issue is on big, huge, contorting, distorting, walloping, scorching, flying, flowing, heaving, wailing, and just generally unbelievable AIR. However, there are also three seriously important things happening in the sport that definitely need to be called to your attention.

The first thing is air that really is unbelievable. You probably know that the trampoline has become an effective training tool for airmasters everywhere. That's fine and good, but it's not so fine and good when somebody takes a photograph of a tramp air and palms it off as real, on-the-hill air. So let it be known that we always make it our policy to use only the cleanest, genuine, untampered with, 100% grade-A air shots in our mag. Don't get blown away by bogus air!

Point number two has to do with the new plastic boards currently making an impact on the market. They're a great inexpensive alternative for young riders and beginners, but since some of them do not have metal edges they should not, repeat not, be used at resorts. If you see an inadequately equipped beginner about to embarass your sport on the slopes, warn him about what he's doing: keep resort management off his (and your) back.

The last point is some good news for everybody: resort acceptance is at an all time high, about 75%. In comparison, it was only 7% when ISM launched its first issue four years ago. The increase is fantastic, except that our resort directory, like The Blob, is wolfing down everything around it. But don't worry—we won't let you suffer from photo deprivation. In the future we may just print a much smaller list of resorts that *don't* allow!

Have a good year, and keep reading ISM—the first mag, the last word.

sary and the days of not having highbacks on bindings or having metal fins on boards were gone. We now had boards with highbacks built in for better forward lean when trying to turn, wraparound metal edges, and kicked up tails for riding backward. Snowboard companies were coming out with new versions of equipment every single season. We were constantly testing prototype models. And suddenly, snowboard companies were a part of the ski industry trade show. They now had a place where they could display snowboard products and write orders with skateboard shops and newly formed snowboard shops.

The new designs in snowboards enabled riders to advance quickly. Tricks that used to take us a whole season to learn were all in a day's worth of practice. Suddenly, pros were popping up on the scene after only riding for a year. Snowboarding was evolving faster than anyone could have imagined and was catching on so quickly that new contests and professional snowboard teams were being formed all over. What's so strange is how schools were blind to this new form of "team." I sometimes envied the soccer and softball teams because they were all together and would wear their jerseys to school on big game days. Everyone knew who the quarterback was, everyone knew the halfback and goalie in soccer. No one knew what a halfpipe freestyler snowboarder was. I was the snowboarder girl, so sometimes I'd wear my GoSkate shirt just to give our sport some props.

In my senior year, even though part of me wanted to go with the flow and follow my friends to the universities, I knew I would end up taking a different path. I already was. I started to think about art colleges and put together my art résumé and a portfolio with my drawings and paintings and some designs I'd made from Jammers surf shorts. I went on many interviews to different kinds of schools for art, fashion design, and graphic design and showed them my portfolio, hoping they saw talent in my work. But I also had my snowboard life.

By my second trip back to the World Championships in Breckenridge in 1988, I had met even more professional snowboarders and people in the new snowboarding industry. George Pappas, who was a top pro, was starting a snowboard company with David Kemper and thought that I might be the only girl able to make it onto their snowboard team. I typed up my snowboarding résumé, which included my contest results, where I'd trained

June 10, 1988

Dear James Salter,

Hi! My name is Tina Basich. I live in Sacramento, California. I have been snowboarding for three years in the Tahoe area. I love to travel and go to as many contests as I can get to. I just graduated from High School and am taking off a year to really get serious about this snowboarding sport! I would like to ride for Kemper and represent Kemper snowboards at as many contests as possible. Here is a list of my results;

1986	Donner Ski Ranch	3rd halfpipe	
1987	Donner Ski Ranch	1st halfpipe 1st slalom	1st overall
1/30/88	Donner Ski Ranch	2nd halfpipe 1st slalom	1st overall
3/12/88	Donner Ski Ranch	1st halfpipe	3rd overall
1987	Shasta	1st halfpipe 1st slalom	1st overall
1988	Shasta	1st halfpipe 2nd slalom	1st overall
1988	Lassen	1st slalom 2nd moguls	1st overall
3/15/87	Worlds - Colorado	6th halfpipe	
1988	Worlds - Colorado	12th slalom 13th giant slalom	
1988	Boreal	1st halfpipe 2nd slalom	1st overall

Could you please get back with me as soon as possible on your thoughts and ideas about the situation and what you have to offer.

Sincerely,

Tina Basich

❄ *My first snowboard résumé.*

in the summer, and how I would be a professional representative of their company, and sent it in right away. The thought of being on a snowboarding team was the ultimate. This would mean more than just free stuff. It would mean getting expenses paid and the opportunity to get photos in ads in the new snowboarding magazines. It was a brand-new opportunity and I could hardly wait for their response. I checked the mail every day for two weeks.

Finally, I got a phone call from George Pappas. He said I'd made it onto the team. It was 1988 and I was just graduating from high school. There was a big decision to be made: accept an art scholarship I'd gotten to study graphic design at Santa Cruz College, or take up Mr. Pappas with my Kemper snowboard contract, which offered me $250 a month for six months and a small expense budget for travel. I asked my parents what I should do, and many of my friends' parents couldn't believe it when they said to follow my heart.

Of course, I chose snowboarding.

❄ *The King of the*
Hill starting gate,
Valdez, Alaska.

team rider

My intention was to take a year off before college and see where my snowboarding adventures would take me. My competition schedule got much heavier and I ended up getting more sponsors to help with my travel money. Being sponsored meant that I was under contract to wear only my sponsors' clothing and gear and that I represented them whenever I was snowboarding. My obligations were to compete in snowboarding competitions and be in photo shoots for media exposure in the new snowboarding magazines. I was getting a free ride to travel the world and snowboard. I wasn't giving this up for anything. I was an athlete—a professional snowboarder.

I was also the only girl on my team, but no one seemed to notice really, and I traveled and did everything they did. I felt like I had to because I knew if girls could see me snowboarding, maybe they'd want to give it a try, too. It's frustrating growing up and hearing people say things like, "Oh, girls aren't interested in that. They don't care about video games, they don't care about car racing, they don't care about riding motocross." It's such an old-school attitude, because we do care. And with our generation, if we see another girl out there doing it, *especially* if it's considered a guy thing, we want to try, too. Maybe the reason more girls don't play football is because there aren't many girl football teams? Not because we don't care. I had to ride and do well in competitions and be in photo shoots not just for myself, but so girls would see this sport and it wouldn't fade for them or take a backseat to guys.

On one of my first major photo shoots with my Kemper team in 1990, I rode the powder in Utah, which would eventually change my riding forever. We went to Snowbird ski resort for the shoot and it snowed a foot every night with light, fluffy powder, and the conditions were unbelievable. But we weren't used to the elevation at 11,000 feet above sea level. Our photographer was a smoker and actually passed out in the tram from the altitude. We let the ski patrol deal with him because as the saying goes, "There are no friends on powder days." Fresh powder runs just cannot wait and must be ridden as soon as possible.

None of us were used to the altitude or the big-mountain riding and vast terrain that was waiting for us. For four days, I rode with my teammates, Dana Nicholson, Matty Goodman, Brett Johnson, JD Platt, Andy Hetzel, and David Dowd, following these guys down runs that were steeper than I was used to. It was all I could do to keep up, but hell if I wasn't going to try. I rode harder and even started to jump cliffs because I had to get the girl shot for the team and besides, the powder provided perfectly soft landings. Our experience was so amazing that the whole team vowed to move to Utah for the next winter season.

So, the following year, when I turned twenty-one, I moved out of the house for the first time. I was definitely ready to be on my own, but when I was packing my car, Utah suddenly seemed so far away. I'd have to pay my own bills. Having my own kitchen would be a real test of my cooking abilities. I was so close to my family and was used to having them to come home to after contests. There would always be someone to tell about my latest adventure and my bed and my stuff were all there for me. Now when I came home, who would be there?

Well, there was Andy Hetzel, who was on the team and was now my boyfriend. I thought he was a cool guy and an excellent rider. We moved with the rest of the team to Utah, but decided to get our own place away from the guys. Thank God because before winter even started, two of the other guys on the team who had also moved to Utah trashed their place with TV dinners piled up in the closet and holes in every wall from wrestling or doing whatever young guys on their own for the first time getting drunk every night do.

With a $5,000 budget from Kemper Snowboards, we had a pretty good setup, but I wanted to make sure I was a professional athlete, so I

total Income

88-89 season

TOTAL INCOME
89-90

Board Sales	275.00
Board Sales	275.00
Board Sales	50.00
Photo incentive Oct 15m 89	150.00
Salary from Kemper	1500.00
Board Sale	
winnings Donner GS 2nd	75.00
freestyle 1st	100.00
winnings OP. Canada Blackomb	150.00
moguls 4th	250.00
photo incentive 15m Dec 40	70.00
Victory Schaal 1st ½ pipe Squaw	25.00
1st Slalom Squaw	1000.00
2nd ½ pipe June mt	1000.00
winning 1st ½ pipe Squaw	800.00
1st Slalom Squaw	750.00
2nd ½ pipe June mt.	750.00
6th G.S.	500.00
award ISKI Squaw	100.00
OP Copper mt Pro 1st ½ pipe winnings	250.00
Victory Schebal	800.00
VarneHar heather Air Show 1st victory ½ pipe	1000.00
3rd victory wistele	1000.00
Soda Springs 1st ½ pipe	600.00
1st Slalom	100.00
victory	150.00
	150.00
Quebec OP total winn.	150.00

bought bookkeeping journals to keep track of my expenses and receipts so I could send in expense reports to Kemper and get reimbursed and show my responsibility as a representative of their company. Not many girls were sponsored professional snowboarders and I wanted to do all I could to show I was up for the challenge—not just in my riding. Feeling grown-up about my own place, I also decorated our apartment, which was filled with thrift store furniture and snowboards lined up in the front room, with my paintings, snowboarding posters, and pictures out of magazines.

Snowbird ski resort sponsored us with season passes, so we got to ride almost every day. My life in Utah was spent on that mountain because the powder snow was unlike anything I'd ever ridden before. We knew all of the secret runs and spots for jumping and we knew where to go to avoid the crowds on the weekends and still get fresh, untracked powder days after a snowstorm. Riding in Utah naturally turned me into what's known as a big-mountain rider—people who ride fast on various kinds of natural terrain rather than manmade snowparks or halfpipes. The terrain pushed my abilities beyond pipe riding because these runs were seriously steep, the powder insanely deep, and this required a whole different style of riding that I was starting to love.

Trying to keep up with Andy made me a better snowboarder, as did the other people I met on that mountain. There were so many great riders in Utah who were after the same thing: fresh, untracked powder runs in deep, light Utah snow. Snowbird resort had a following of snowboarders who were not all pros, just riders who snowboarded every single day of the winter. There were people from all over the country who had moved there to be ski lift operators for the season or wait tables in the resort restaurants at night just for the chance for a free ski pass and the ability to ride that mountain. There was a cult-like following of all kinds of people who rode religiously—Lori Gibbs, who became a top racer and big-mountain rider; Natalie Murphy, who went into designing for Quiksilver;

Jane Mouser, who became a designer for Helly Hansen. They lived the lifestyle, too. But in my job, on my team, I was responsible for doing things like jumping cliffs for photo shoots.

The guys I rode with would usually take big airs off cliffs quicker than I would. They'd approach a cliff jump and yell down to someone in the landing zone asking if it was clear and then just go for it. I guess I need to see where I'm going first. If I was too scared to just jump it, I would scope the landing and tell myself that after another snowstorm, when the landing filled in a little bit more, I would try the jump then. But sometimes this would mean I would miss out on the photo shoot because I took too long and I didn't want to be that lame girl snowboarder.

Personally, I think girls are more protective of their bodies and just naturally smarter about risk. It took me longer to calculate and decide if I was going to take the jump or not. I was constantly trying to push my snowboarding. So, to make up for taking too much time scouting, I would often take runs by myself and look at the jumps that I knew we were going to be filming in the next day or so and check them out a little closer. Ride to the edge, look down. Then ride around to the bottom and look up, judging the distance and the impact of the landing. That way when the team rolled up to the jump for the shoot, I already knew what the chances were for me clearing it or sticking the landing.

My lifestyle meant I wasn't always in Utah but traveling for competitions and other photo shoots and rarely in one place for very long. I was on the road more than I was home, which made relationships with guys unusual to say the least. As a professional snowboarder, I never had the typical dating experience like, "Want to go out Friday night, dinner and a movie?" It was more like, "Hey, are you headed out to Breckenridge next weekend?" or "You going to the U.S. Open in Vermont? OK, see you there..." and in those situations, a few so-called dates on the road can sometimes only add to the pressure that already exists at the competition. When I was dating Andy, we were on the same snowboarding

Getting out of the heli in Alaska.

team and traveling together to all of the contests. You would think that two professional snowboarders dating would be a perfect match, but it was too much pressure having our relationship wrapped up into one big combination of snowboarding contests, the same group of friends, the same sponsors, living together, and all the while trying to have a hold of our own parts of it. We were both competing for the same thing: attention from the same sponsors, competition results, and trying to get as many media photos in the mags as possible. Thing is, as a girl, and the only girl on the team, I felt like I had to at least do everything the guys were doing to stay in the game. Not only did I have to get big air jumping cliffs and ride fast and hang with the guys, but be cool, pretty, and feminine. For example, I liked riding with my ponytail flying behind me so there was no question of my femininity. I was proud to be a snowboarder girl. But that balance of being a great rider and a girl was schizophrenic, and there were only a handful of girls out there who were supposedly doing that dance right. Plus, when you're twenty-two years old, you're constantly striving for your own independence. There were some months during my winters when I would only be home four days out of the whole month. That's hard on any relationship, and we ended up breaking up.

However, I had an unconditional relationship with the snow in Utah. When you feel the powder fields in Utah under your feet, flying through them and creating sparkling white diamond plumes with each turn down the mountain, you're light as a feather, and it makes you love this feeling. It's as if you're not even touching the ground, and sometimes it seems as though the only reason the snowline is there below you is to remind you that you're still on earth. It was unlike anywhere else I had ever ridden and it was the best big-mountain riding I knew of. Those experiences kept me there and one season turned into nine. In the summers, I'd come home to Sacramento to see friends and family, or ride up at Mt. Hood, Oregon, and practice for the upcoming World Cup tour in the halfpipe. In the winters, I'd spend as much time as I could riding fresh powder in what felt like my home state, whenever I wasn't traveling to compete with my team. I was feeling so confident in my abilities when I rode Utah because where on earth could there be better snow or more diverse terrain or challenges like this here, on my mountain?

But there was another place. A bigger place. Alaska. Other snowboarders on my team were talking about it. There were stories from other competitors and friends about the endless, untracked powder fields accessible only by seaplane or helicopter. They said you could land on unknown peaks that rocketed 5,000 feet up and you could ride right down to the sea. But no one owned Alaska or called Alaska their mountain. No one would dare and I didn't really know why. It was kind of mysterious—people would say you have to see it for yourself.

Some of my team members, including my brother, were talking about heading up there in 1995 for this new freeriding contest called "King of the Hill." To me, Alaska seemed so far away and very intimidating. Eskimos lived there in igloos and spearfished, right? Plus, how could

I ever pack for this one? But my Kemper team was going and as part of the team, I headed with them for my first real backcountry experience.

This place checked my snowboarding reality fast. My first couple of trips up there, I snowboarded the worst I'd ever ridden. Alaska is so intimidating. Unlike a ski resort, there are no boundaries or clearly marked trails and warnings about cliffs and crevasses or shallow snow. It's up to you to learn the mountain you're riding. Alaska is Mother Nature at her most extreme—the weather changes quickly, snow conditions can change within one run—it's vast and steep and bigger than all of us.

The Kemper team, 1989.

King of the Hill was held in Valdez, Alaska, which to the world is known for its oil spill. To us, Valdez is known as the Mecca of helicopter snowboarding for powder. The idea for the competition was really cool for freeriders—people like myself who liked to ride different terrain on big mountains. The concept was to challenge a snowboarder's freeriding skills through two different big-mountain runs: one run was timed, one judged. Each run had different types of terrain, such as cornices, rocky cliffbands, and windlips in the snowbanks that served as natural jumps. So truly the best overall rider would win in each division—male and female. The combination of the two scores determined who was crowned the King or Queen of the Hill.

The extreme competition runs already were almost too much to think about. I wasn't sure if I knew how to ride all of those conditions even though I was pretty good in Utah, and it didn't help that the final competition run was named "School Bus" because of its "educating terrain." I didn't want to be schooled in Alaska. The contest was purposely challenging a true test—and accessible only by helicopter. But when I got there, it proved to be even more overwhelming, with helicopters and seaplanes flying around serving as transportation to and from the tops of the mountain peaks. Skiers and snowboarders with backpacks full of backcountry gear like ropes, small avalanche shovels, ice picks, and crevasse safety harnesses populated the small fishing town. The weather was always the topic of conversation because helicopters and planes could only fly on fair-weather days, which would determine whether or not we got a chance to ride because there were no ski resorts around. In Alaska, fair-weather days were few and far between. You could ask any snowboarder, and on cue they could hum the jingle to the Weather Channel. That's why I always travel with my paint set. It's nice to have with me on those down days when I'm stuck in my hotel room because of bad weather. I need more options than room service and Pay-Per-View. It's nice to just turn on some music and paint. Sometimes I'd just nerd-out and bring my knitting with me, but since September 11, that's one thing I've had to leave behind.

To get to the top of a run in Alaska, you have to take a helicopter ride up the mountain. I'd never been in a helicopter before and I was more than nervous. I felt sick. I was also unprepared—I didn't have a backcountry gear backpack or even water with me. All I had was a Power-Bar. The thunder of the helicopter blades and the smell of the exhaust got my heart pumping from both fear and adrenaline. During the first ride up to the peak, I didn't even enjoy the amazing view because I was too busy staring at all the blinking lights on the console and watching the pilot.

Exiting the helicopter at the top of the mountain was wild. The wind from the rotor-wash blasted snow into my face and it was a total white-out until the helicopter lifted off and left us on the peak. All of a sudden it was quiet and we were by ourselves in the middle of nowhere and on our own to make our way down the mountain. I was thankful that at least my brother was there. It was such a comfort to have him traveling with me. It made me feel safer.

The top of the mountain was so much colder than down at the heli-pad and I hadn't brought extra clothing like an experienced backcountry rider would have. But I was wearing an avalanche beacon, which is a trans-ceiver used for search and rescue, in case I was buried in an avalanche. Still, I was numb to these dangers. Down below, I hadn't thought it was really possible that I would be in an avalanche. And I had never even seen one before. At the top, on that lone peak, the reality was much different and I felt this new danger.

During the King of the Hill competition, I was surrounded again by my peers who were also feeling the shock of new surroundings. The start-ing gate was intimidating because the first thing I had to do was jump off a cornice—a thick slab of snow overhanging the top of the moun-tain—just to start my first run. There was one small way to go around it if someone chose to do that, but I didn't want to be the competitor who skipped the cornice. Plus it wouldn't be good for my score. So to start my run off strongly, I dropped in. I had my hair in braids, and later, photos in magazines would caption me dropping in as "Pippi Rides the Bus in Alaska" because my hair was flying under my blue helmet. I went for a straight, fast line in the middle of School Bus, cut back skier's right, then dropped a cliffband that I'd scouted from the helicopter. From down below where the judges were looking up through binoculars, they probably couldn't see if I'd stuck the landing but would know if I didn't come into view within a few seconds. Luckily, it was soft like Utah; I landed it and rode on. I made big swooping S's down a steep powder field that led into a series of windlips and I finally got the courage to use one as a jump and catch air at the bottom. This completed my run, but I didn't ride my best. I think everyone else was in the same frame of mind. I missed coming in first place that first year by just one point, coming in second to Julie Zell, who was an experienced big-mountain rider from Jackson Hole, Wyoming. But I thought, did that mean I was Princess of the Hill with second place? I'd take it. King of the Hill got me up there riding Alaska. And that trip made me realize I had a lot more to learn about snowboarding.

how to get sponsored

1. Get on your snowboard as much as possible. The more comfortable you are the better you will perform.

2. Enter a contest and show your stuff. No matter where you are, if you are rippin' at a contest someone will notice. Reps from companies and other sponsored riders are always keeping their eyes open for new talent. Don't get discouraged if you fall or suck the first time around. Take it all for the experience and it can lead to so much more.

3. Meet people and reps who might have leads to free stuff and hookups.

4. Write letters to companies addressed to team managers asking about their sponsorship program; include any photos of yourself riding, and a list of contest results and goals.

5. Don't get discouraged if you don't get what you want. You might not get the full ride right off the bat—maybe only a small sponsorship with some gear—but be grateful for everything you get because that attitude can take you far.

6. A great place to meet reps and pros are at local demos and events. Don't be shy—go around and introduce yourself. Sometimes it's all about who you know and showing your enthusiasm for the sport.

Most of the time companies want you to prove yourself first, so if you get a free board or a free T-shirt, wear it with pride next time you go snowboarding. Companies want great people representing their goods and people who are proud of their sponsorship. ✳

❄ *Checking out the*
view in Alaska.

WOMENS TEAM 2000.
KIM BOHNSACK • TINA BASICH • TARA DAKIDES

SIMS
SNOWBOARDS

*The girls team
appears in a
Sims ad, 2000.*

girls on
the scene

Taking a year off from college wasn't happening as long as I could keep this snowboarding career going. I was never going back to college full time. I used my extra time in the summers to take crash courses in graphic design and photography, realizing my other interests could be used in my snowboarding career. My competition results and accomplishments grew stronger as my riding got better and more diverse. I started taking snowboarding more seriously because I was eager to gain respect and represent my sponsors as a professional athlete. Snowboarding was turning into my career.

During this time in the early '90s, there was a big change happening for women in many sports, including tennis, golf, soccer, skiing. There was a global movement going on and women were getting more attention. It wasn't just girls in snowboarding who were finally being recognized; women were stepping up and showing off their stuff. Sports were becoming a major part of our lives. They were empowering in so many ways. They weren't just a hobby that we did for fitness anymore.

Just twenty years earlier, sports were not even offered to girls in high school. My mom was a cheerleader and for women of her generation this was the only active program available. I read this story once that really moved me and made me realize what women have been through. In 1972 a woman named K. Switzer ran in the then men-only Boston Marathon. Race officials actually tried to force her off the course. She finished the 26.4-mile race and from that point on she ran marathons in a dress to make a statement that women are athletes too. Actions like these changed how women were accepted in sports. We were the result of an evolution for women in sports that was only just the beginning.

My generation was lucky because we had soccer, softball, track, and other sports available to choose from. We didn't even have to think about *not* having sports. That would have been so unfair. Plus, we saw female professional athletes in magazines and on TV in tennis, gymnastics, ice skating, and basketball. It was possible. Being a strong female athlete was a statement—not new but different and very strong and respectable. We were part of a generation of women allowed to think that way—that sports could be a fierce, strong statement and an independent career. In my generation, when we see other girls succeeding in sports, we don't think, "I can't do that." It's more like, "If she can, I can too." That's how we think. Anything is possible.

With our participation in contests, more and more girls started snowboarding and getting involved. In the earlier years, there was a handful of girls at each contest. One handful. Over the years, that number kept growing. There was a chain reaction. Not only was the number of girls in the sport growing, but we also had girls in the industry or business side. There was Lisa Hudson who worked at Airwalk, one of my first sponsors, plus Gaylene Nagel working at Sims, Darcy Lee at Cold As Ice apparel, Monica Steward at Bonfire snowboard clothing, Kathleen Gasperini at *Snow-*

boarder magazine. It was a combination of the girls in the industry and the athletes that really was the key formula for making such a strong representation. Without these women, our place in snowboarding would never have been so prevalent. They helped create our culture and show the world what we had going on.

I now had other female snowboarders to look up to because there were more women competing, even though it was still a male-dominated sport. These girls pushed me to ride harder because we now realized that younger girls would follow, too, and we no longer had the excuse of being the only girl in the group. My first major event in Tahoe, the OP Pro at Squaw Valley back in 1990, had all the big-name Tahoe girls like Bonnie Learey, Roberta Rogers, my friends Angie Dominguez and Heather Mills. Plus, the girls from Utah and Colorado—Jean Higgins, Susie Riggins, and Lori Gibbs. I had competed against these girls in Colorado at the World Championships but now I had a few tricks I could do in the halfpipe and I was eager to see how I stood up to the competition. Riding and competing in the halfpipe was my favorite discipline. I never got into the racing side of snowboarding because it was too much like skiing, which represented what everyone else was doing and I wanted to be different, trying new tricks and pushing the level of the sport. I love the feeling of catching air and doing tricks. It was fun to get a jam session going with a group of snowboarders and try new ones. Because snowboarding was less than ten years old, we were curious to see how those tricks would score at the next competition.

Jean Higgins was new on the scene and the girl to beat. She was known for trying a new trick called a J-tear, an inverted flip with a half twist. Jean had perfected her J-tears to the point where she was flipping them at the end of the pipe, and even though she wasn't quite landing them yet, it was a big deal and earned her big points in competition. That day on my halfpipe run, I pulled off my layback stall on the frontside wall, an ally-oop on my backside wall, and a 180-to-fakie (ending backward) at

❄ *Rocking the halfpipe.*

the end of the pipe. I finished my run knowing it was going to be a close finish with Jean Higgins's score. They announced it over the loudspeaker that I'd won by two points. I was so excited and my mom and dad were there cheering for me, which meant so much more.

While I was best at the freestyle event, I still entered all disciplines at that contest. We all did. Nobody had focused on specializing in one discipline yet. I remember surprisingly making it to the finals of the dual slalom. I was at the top of the starting gate getting ready to compete head-to-head against Lori Gibbs. She was from Utah and like so many girls from Utah, was an excellent big-mountain rider, too. She was also known to be a fast racer. She had all the right gear, a race board, hard boots, and racing pads. Of course I didn't have any of the proper equipment for racing. I was a freestyle rider and most comfortable on my freestyle board, which had a flipped-up tail for going backward, unlike an asymmetrical race board, and softer boots and bindings. I had a Domino's pizza box wrapped around my arm as a gate protection pad (we'd order pizza the night before so we could make our "gear" for dual slalom race days). Lori slammed her race board down in the starting gate and looked over at me and said, "Let's see what you got, Basich."

Talk about pressure. At first I was so intimidated, mainly because of her slick gear. Riding in a Domino's pizza box was not exactly as glamorous as her ergonomic, tricked-out body pads. But whenever someone says something that challenges me, or makes me feel like a punk skater from Sac in the middle of a football party, something inside rises up and I start burning. I thought, "I'm going to go fast and show you what I got." I had only competed against Lori a few times before and had never been fast enough to beat her. But on this day, we were going head-to-head for first and second place, Racer vs. the Halfpipe Rider.

It was a close race because I lucked out. She fell in our first run and that gave me a 1.5-second advantage. On our second run all I had to do was stay within 1.5 seconds behind her. I went fast and my Domino's box completely ripped off my arm, but I knew I had won as I passed through the finish line right after her. It was a big moment for me. I received the overall award, plus my two first places in slalom and halfpipe at the contest. I now had three more trophies to add to my shelf. My walls were covered with snowboard posters and banners from my sponsors. I had stickers on my windows and door, and each of my medals carefully hung above my desk.

Snowboarding at this point was a big part of my entire family's lives. I think my competitions and efforts to do well and getting to know other snowboarders inspired Michael also. We watched each other compete and talked about new tricks and had some of the same friends. For him, snowboarding was a huge help with his confidence, something he was good at, a way to express himself. He was back in school after three years of home school and wanted to be with his other classmates. He had overcome epilepsy and wasn't having seizures and was motivated to learn and catch up with his reading and writing so he could send in his résumé and get his own sponsors.

For myself, competing in all disciplines against America's best female snowboarders prepared me for the next step of competitive snowboarding. With my list of podium standings, I was qualified to compete in the newly developed World Cup tour, which traveled through Europe and Japan. My accomplishments also lead to more contracts with sponsors. I was getting paid more as an athlete to snowboard, which meant I had to perform and do well on the World Cup circuit against the world's best. The more we got together to compete, the higher the bar was raised. We were pulling tricks that seemed highly unlikely in the beginning years—among guys or girls. One thing's for sure, skiers were no longer saying we weren't athletes. It even started a whole new movement in skiing and new "freestyle skiers" were starting to copy our moves.

Shannon, Michele Taggart,
and me at the Op Pro Contest.

❄ *Traveling
with all of
our team gear.*

world traveler

In 1992, with the support of my sponsors Kemper, Airwalk, Smith, and OP, I traveled to Europe for my first World Cup series contest. My travel plans were set up by our team manager at Kemper Snowboards. The distributors in each country offered to help us with transportation and lodging arrangements, but even with all that taken care of, I was in culture shock from everything I saw. It was nice to be traveling with my team, which included my brother, but this was my first trip overseas and everything was overwhelming, including the snow and the mountains.

In Europe the mountains are huge and the resorts do not always mark all the natural hazards and boundaries. You could ride off a cliff or go the wrong way into a valley where you'd have to hike out because there is no lift access to that area. It was nothing like Donner Ski Ranch or Breckenridge in Colorado. Not to mention the fact that I had never traveled by train before and with the language barrier, it was hard enough to get from the airport to the hotel with two huge duffel bags and a snowboard bag of gear that would never fit well in the trains, let alone get from the hotel to the mountain and try to find the halfpipe *on* the mountain in time for practice. I was quick to learn the ways of Europe because I had no other choice. There were more and more sponsored riders, so we had a good-sized-group of Americans competing in the World Cup together, but for some American snowboarders, it really knocked their confidence because things were just so different. For me, it was definitely hard to stay confident, but I didn't mind the new cultures and I liked talking with people with different accents and hearing the things they had to say. I'd learned very early on, from the Option Institute and my parents and Michael, about not being judgmental, so I think it was easier for me to be open to different kinds of people. I liked talking to foreigners (although we were the foreigners). I liked their accents and how musical French and Italian sounded, and I liked how they used their hands so much. I could even pick up on a few words from my years taking German and Spanish at Waldorf, which was helpful.

But in European competitions, I had the feeling that the judges were biased to their riders. The competition was tough and the European girls were good, but we were also really good. European riders were mostly known for their racing backgrounds, not freestyle. Americans were the freestyle experts—we invented halfpipe riding—and there was this national pride thing going on with us. We had to make sure we owned what we had invented. My bag of tricks was expanding to frontside 540s and handplants, but European girls were pushing the level of tricks in the pipe, too, and on new equipment I'd never seen before. They had snowboard brands like Crazy Banana and Checkered Pig. Their snowboard outfits were very fashionable with more patterns and flowers or checkering. Plus, they seemed smarter because they could often speak three languages and already had stories of traveling the world, or at least Europe,

🌸 *Snowboarding
in August at Valle
Nevado, Chile, 1994.*

which seemed like another world to me. So at the top of the pipe, it was like this group from other countries and then the Americans. They could talk to each other and could communicate among different countries. We couldn't understand them unless they spoke English to us. We were the outsiders. And it was sometimes so disappointing because I'd travel so far and perform my best and not even make my usual top five spots. That took some getting used to.

On one trip to the World Cup in Ishgal, Austria, professional snowboarder and best friend Shannon Dunn and I arrived five days early to adjust to the time change and get prepared for the contest. We were determined to get into the top three and we thought putting in the extra effort was going to make the difference. We had our tricks that we wanted to pull off listed on a piece of paper like a checklist. We practiced every day. We thought we were ready, but on the day of the contest we both fell on our first qualifying runs. We didn't even get as far as the finals. Out of thirty girls competing, Shannon finished second to last and I ended up absolutely last. It really sucks reading your name at the bottom of a list, posted on a big white board for the entire European snowboarding community to read. I didn't dare tell people we'd come early or mention our so-called preparations. We walked back to our hotel with our boards under our arms, trying not to listen to other riders—the winners—talking in foreign languages, and we were instantly overcome with a feeling of being homesick. We wanted to get out of there, back to the States, where we always did our best on our home turf. At the hotel, we funneled into the four-person elevator with about ten other competitors. The doors closed and someone mentioned that there were too many people in there. Some obnoxious Euro guy started jumping up and down, yelling something in French, to scare everyone and the elevator suddenly dropped about 10 feet. The lights flickered out and we ended up crammed in there in the dark for two hours while the extremely angry Austrian hotel maintenance men tried to get the doors open. Finally, they got them open and we crawled out between two floors.

When the hotel management saw how many of us were in there, they started yelling at us in German and wouldn't give us our passports back when we tried to check out. Instead, they made us pay $1,400 for the repair. The Euro guys took off—we didn't know most of them—and Shannon and I were stuck with the bill. The responsible girls. We finally coughed it up because we thought at this point we would never get home. I was hoping Kemper would accept the bill as an expense on my report, but they weren't buying it at all. We were so pissed at those guys. But for some reason, experiences like that just fueled the fire and we kept at it, going back to Europe to compete and gain the respect from the girls on the World Cup—many of whom later became my close friends.

Competing in Japan on the World Cup tour, however, was a different story, mainly because it seemed like we were respected right off the bat. Snowboarding was a new sport in Japan, and the level of riding there was

✳ *An indoor ski resort in Japan, 1996.*

overpowered by U.S. and European riders. There was at least one stop on the World Cup tour in Japan every winter and I always looked forward to those trips because they were such a unique experience. Japan was a new world in a different way than Europe. For one thing, traveling on our own was not even an option because you can't even try to read the signs at the train station, let alone on the mountain, because the alphabet is different characters and everything reads right to left. It always freaked me out to see all of these kids reading comics, starting with what seemed like the last page and flipping forward. And when I got the "cover" shot of a Japanese snowboard magazine, it seemed like it was on the back, not the front. It was very cool, but obviously weird for a girl from Sac.

The Japanese distributor of our snowboard sponsor took us around from the start of the trip until the end. Thankfully we had a guided tour. I used to think that American cities had a lot of vending machines and automated high-tech systems, but *everything* is automated in Japan. You can buy a 40-ounce beer out of a vending machine on any street corner. There's even an indoor ski resort! When I first saw it, from the outside it looked like a high-rise building lying on its side and held up by scaffolding. What a crazy experience to ride a ski lift up an indoor mountain and snowboard under huge lights rather than the sky. It was like a big ice chest and set up like a roller rink: Rent your skis and head on in for your three-hour session.

Although it took a few trips before I understood the true experience of Japan, I always loved the oddball things that would happen to me there, like the time during a promotional appearance when this guy asked Shannon and me to sign his car and another couple wanted us to sign their rice cooker. We also saw a Mercedes parked in front of a skyscraper in downtown Tokyo with a brand-new snowboard attached permanently to the ski rack—a total fashion statement.

Snowboards were selling like hotcakes, so the Japanese distributors were generous and paid for our trips for promotions and snowboarding contests. The Japanese market was strong and boards were selling for around $850 (the same boards sold in the U.S. for $400). We couldn't believe it. After one shop appearance a distributor took Shannon and me shopping and we noticed that we were being followed. Two Japanese schoolgirls would hide behind vending machines as we came out of stores and just stare at us. This happened all afternoon until finally our distributor went up to them to see what they wanted. He brought the girls over to us and I said in my broken Japanese, "Nice to meet you." The taller girl burst into tears. My distributor taught me how to say "It's OK" (dishobu). They were completely flipping out because they were fans of ours. I couldn't believe it. I had a true fan! We talked with them for ten minutes with our distributor translating and I gave the tall girl my address. A year later, I received a letter from her saying she was starting to learn to read and write in English so she could send me a letter. Two years later on a trip to Japan for the World Cup, I saw her again. This time she had a laminated picture of me around her neck. That's so extreme, but that's how Japan is—anything can happen and when it does, it goes Richter.

I don't eat fish, so on my first trip to Japan I thought that eating would be impossible. Everyone I had talked to who had been to Japan said "I hope you like fish," so I had visions of nothing but raw fish and I packed about twenty Cup-a-Soups in my duffel bag, thinking I could always find hot water to add to make soup. This was how I was going to survive. Funny that in Japan, Cup-a-Soups are sold in every corner market. I looked at the labels of the Cup-a-Soups that I'd brought from Sacramento and they were all imported from Japan! I was clueless. No matter what anyone tells you, in Japan there are so many different kinds of interesting food and I ended up finding many that I liked. My favorite was the Korean BBQ (alright, so it's Korean...) where you cook everything yourself on a grill built into the table, which guaranteed me that I wasn't going to eat anything raw.

I've been to Japan about fifteen times now and I'm still learning to say things correctly in their language. I would try to learn one word on each trip, making lists of translated words in my journal. The culture and people are amazing and they take to new things immediately. Snowboarding was one of their passions and from the beginning, they were eager to learn more about the American snowboarding style. It was almost an obsession for them. Within a few years on World Cup, the Japanese riders were stepping up in competitions and creating their own heroes, like my friend Tomoko Yamakoshi, who is now one of Japan's top pros and one of the top coaches at Girlfriends Camp in Japan. Snowboarding in Japan exploded as a sport and was considered very cool. Meanwhile, their pros gained recognition on the World Cup scene in only a few years. Now, top ten contenders on the circuit always include riders from Japan.

I was becoming a world traveler and when winter was over in North America, our sponsors would send us south of the equator for photo shoots, to Chile, New Zealand, and Australia, where it was winter.

❄ *Loving the backcountry in Utah.*

On a trip with my Kemper team in Australia, I ended up the envy of all the guys, not because of my riding skills but because of who I ended up riding with. This was a new mountain and I was having a hard time keeping up with the guys on the team, like Steve Graham and Dave Dowd, so I went and rode by myself. There was a guy in the liftline who was also snowboarding by himself. He was all bundled up in goggles and a coat with his collar turned up, wearing a hat pulled way down because it was snowing pretty heavily. We started riding together, which is really no big deal, because we were on the same runs and we kept running into each other in the liftline. I rode a few more runs with him and then decided to take a break for lunch and he split. I headed into the lodge to meet up with the guys from my team and they said, "Hey, someone said that Adam from the Beastie Boys is here snowboarding. He has green hair."

After lunch, I went back out to my runs and my buddy that I'd ridden with in the morning was there so I ended up riding with him for the rest of the day. I invited him to come hang out with my friends for drinks after the lifts closed. He came in with me and my friends all said hi. Then he took off his goggles and hat and we just stared. He had green hair.

Adam Yauch became a great friend and ended up being my roommate in Utah for a couple of seasons. He would even come out in between recording albums to get in some powder turns. He had the same passion for snowboarding that we did. He rode with us at Snowbird and whenever his band played in the area, he would hook us up with like fifty passes for all the Utah snowboarder locals. Then, we'd all go riding the next day.

It was a group effort, riding in new places and figuring things out like getting to competitions and actually competing. It's funny when the only words you can understand over the loudspeaker in exotic locations are the names of snowboard tricks being announced. This was pre-Olympics. There were no coaches telling us what to do or driving us around to and from the mountain or checking us into airports and hotels. Being on the road takes you away from your home and family, so my teammates became my support group, and my circle of closest friends were often the girls I'd compete against around the world. Unlike the days when I was the only girl, I liked the fact that I could meet up with women on the competition circuit. It was comforting to talk about things like having a snowboarder boyfriend versus *not* having a snowboarder boyfriend (which was never really clear). We'd talk about the latest tricks we were trying and the differences in our equipment. We'd talk about competing during a day of having insanely debilitating cramps. I clearly remember the sense of kinship I felt in the starting area of a pipe competition in Austria when I casually mentioned to Shannon how I'd been popping Midol all day and hoped I could pull it together. The girl from Sweden behind me said, "Me too."

Sometimes we'd rally a group of girls together and just go ride in the trees far away from any halfpipe. We'd push each other at our own paces and stop and take group pictures at the top of the mountain for my journal. Other girls had journals, too, and would draw or write about their lives like I did. Some of these girls were so creative—artists and poets writing about their adventures in different countries. It's comforting to have that group of girls on the road, traveling with you to competitions or meeting up at events and sharing tips, like never wear an underwire bra (crashes cause boob bruises). We also turned to each other for support in dealing with injuries or jet lag. Someone was always carrying the Advil or Arnica in her coat, and we often had the worst shin splints from riding the halfpipe five days a week. The big joke was Who's got the Tiger Balm this trip? This was my world and these were my best friends.

travel tips

* **People who don't travel a lot may not**
realize how gross it is to sleep in hotel sheets for days in
a row and eat at restaurants and use public phones all the
time. Cell phones take care of the latter these days, but here
are some travel tips I've learned from being on the road as
a professional snowboarder.

 I travel with a little set of chopsticks, so if I'm uncomfortable
eating from not-so-clean silverware in not-so-clean
restaurants, I bust out my little chopsticks. I actually got
my chopsticks at the Tokyo Disneyland, and they have this
little case and a Mickey Mouse on them, but whatever. You
can get chopsticks these days pretty easily. So, whenever
I travel and start getting grossed out, I bust out the
chopsticks.

Whenever I order a drink I always ask for a straw, which is
usually clean and fresh, instead of sipping on the lipstick
prints from some old lady who drank from that glass before
you.

When you're flying in an airplane and you get up from your
seat, don't grab the seat in front of you. There's nothing
worse than trying to sleep and someone's jarring your seat
to get up, so be courteous of other people.

🛏 I always bring my own pillowcase to put over the pillow in a hotel room. Or if you don't have one, you can use a T-shirt so that you have your cheeks against your own nice fabric.

☣ When staying at hotels, always check the bed before you hop into it. Take off the bedspread and put it into the closet because hotels don't wash those. They're a dry-clean-only item, and I'll bet the hotels only clean them once a year if we are lucky. I saw the HBO special that showed what's actually on those bedspreads and it ain't pretty. So for me they go right into the closet first thing. I just sit on the sheets—at least they wash those.

🌸 I always bring my essential oil kit with me. In hotels in Japan and Vegas, for example, the windows don't open, so you can get claustrophobic with totally recycled air constantly being pumped in. I bring cotton balls and dab a little lavender on one and stick it in the air-conditioning vent. It filters into the air and you don't feel like you're stuck breathing the same air. This is also a good tip for people who have to travel a lot in traffic—you can put the cotton ball in your car vent and the exhaust fumes won't bother you as much. I also bring lemon and peppermint oil for restaurant water because it's usually tap water and tastes horrible. Add a few drops of peppermint and you have flavored water that tastes pretty good. ✳

CHAPTER 9

BOARDING FOR **BREAST CANCER**

BREAST SELF EXAM shower card

The single most important tool for surviving breast cancer is EARLY DETECTION.

WHY DO IT?

Get to know yourself. Nobody knows your body better than you.

Check yourself out in the mirror and ask yourself these questions.
Do my breasts look the same?
Is one larger or smaller than the other?
Are my nipples the same shape?
Are the veins more noticeable on one breast than the other?
Is there any rippling of the skin, bruises or bulges?

EXAM: HOW TO DO IT!

STEP 1 You can do a breast exam either lying down or standing up. Either way use the fleshy pads of your first three fingers of opposite hand.

STEP 2 Examine entire breast area, from your armpit to below your breast.

STEP 3 Take your first 3 fingers and make 3 circles – light, medium & firm pressure around breast area. Walk your fingers from area to area – don't lift them off the breast.

Starting at the breastbone, you can either move fingers up and down the breast or circle around the breast. Remember to include the armpit area.

STEP 4

STEP 5 When you're done with the touch test, gently squeeze your nipples. You are looking for any breast discharge or pain

Do this every month to become familiar with your own body and what is normal for you. Best time to do a breast exam? Ten days after your period when tenderness and swelling are low.

If you notice any changes or feel pain, call your doctor and schedule an appointment.

PAUL FRANK
paul frank industries

BOARDING FOR **BREAST CANCER**

PAUL FRANK
supports **BOARDING FOR BREAST CANCER**

EXAM.

HEN YOUR BREASTS ARE ES FROM AGES 10-16.

RY MONTH.

F LESS COMMON T BREAST CANCER. EN WITH THIS DISEASE

YOUR PERIOD.

IS COMMON Y IN YOUNG WOMEN.

hould you do BSE anyway?

COMMON AMONG SLIGHTLY DIFFERENT

TS. IN FACT, Y WOMEN DOING

AN'S PARTNER ER.

outh dation. cer, the y lifestyle.

vention

boarding for
breast cancer

hannon Dunn and I traveled together a lot, competing at the same events. We were both doing well in our competitions around the world and riding progressively on our boards, but we were also ready to make our mark in the industry in other ways. Our sponsors knew that we were highlights of their snowboard teams, and in 1994 we were the first girls to release signature pro model snowboards. She had the Shannon Dunn board by Sims and I had the Tina Basich board by Kemper. We were able to help design the boards to our specifications and design our own art for the graphics. It was the perfect opportunity to tie in my art with my snowboarding career. I remember finding a list of goals that I had made a few years earlier that listed "My own pro model snowboard" with a "ha-ha!" next to it. At the time I thought it was a long shot because only guys had pro model snowboards. I was proving myself wrong and that became a big deal in so many ways. Professional and Olympic women skiers were shocked. It turned the heads of corporate sports manufacturers like Nike and Trek. Other than basketball shoes and tennis rackets, not many other manufacturers had professional female-endorsed sporting equipment.

The snowboarding industry completely embraced our efforts, and to our surprise, even guys were riding our boards. It really shook up the industry and sparked a new wave of female athlete–endorsed equipment.

While my first pro model was in 1994 with Kemper, my first hand-painted board graphics were in 1995 when I moved to Sims. Shannon called me and said she was leaving Sims for Burton so there was a spot open on the Sims snowboard team. Kemper was struggling to stay in business at the time, so I called Sims and they flew me up to Canada right away to the main office. I had a big meeting, which is where I first met Gaylene Nagel, who was the marketing and team director. Sims said, "OK, we want you on our team, and we're going to give you a pro model snowboard, and we need your graphics by tomorrow." The meeting went just like that. I was so stoked for this new opportunity. Sims was a big company and I wanted to make this deal work.

I had my paint set with me and I went back to my hotel room and painted all night, then FedExed my graphics to the Sims factory in Europe the next day. I'd painted a watercolor of a butterfly fairy. From that point on, I've always been able to have my artwork on my pro models with Sims snowboards, which is one of the reasons why it was such an accomplishment for me—not only to finally have my own signature board, but to have my art under my feet throughout the winter.

But clothing was still a problem area. I always wore guys' snowboarding outfits because there was no other choice and nothing ever fit. I'd have to roll up the sleeves and the pants and wear a belt to hold them up. This was the "baggy pants big stance" era, meaning oversized jackets and pants were in style, but we were wearing guys' oversized gear that was twice as big. My pants would get stuck in my bindings and sometimes

I'd do a trick in the pipe only to have my coat ride up and blind my view for the landing. Oversized was only cool to a point. We were pro riders and needed clothing that fit, and the monster clothing was getting in the way. Plus, the demand for women-specific equipment and apparel was increasing because more girls and women were getting into snowboarding. New girls would not be into the dark browns, blacks and big, oversized jackets and pants. Honestly, we looked so far from being feminine.

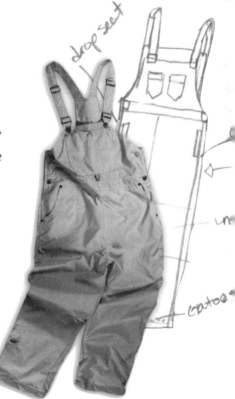

Shannon and I were lucky that Lisa Hudson, who worked at Sway snowboard clothing, also saw there was a need for change and came to encourage us to get more involved in designing our own line of women's snowboard clothing. She was the driving force in the outerwear business to get manufacturers and designers to accept and understand the need for functional, feminine girls' apparel. I was all over it. Like designing my Jammers surf trunks and my prom dress, this was a chance to take it way further and for real. Lisa set up the funding with investors and I dove into learning the process of design and production. We'd have "design meetings" where I'd show Lisa and Shannon my colored line drawings of outfits. I really wanted to make this happen and so did Shannon. This wasn't just me and my buddies using my mom's sewing machine anymore, this was about sourcing waterproof fabrics, choosing color swatches, and testing designs for movement and freedom.

In 1994, we launched a women's line from Swag called Prom, which was the second women's clothing line out there for girl snowboarders. We were ready to look like girls and Lisa helped make it happen, allowing us the freedom to design clothes with slimmer cuts, pastel colors, and butterfly logos. We were as girly as we wanted to be and rocked it with confidence. Our Prom ads were completely revolutionary for snowboarding: We wore prom dresses to show that we weren't afraid to be feminine. Our apparel line was a crossover from snowboarding to our lifestyle and it really represented who we were becoming: grown professional female snowboarders.

It made an impression on the snowboarding industry—a women's movement, we would later call it. It was the push in women's apparel that helped start more manufacturers to design women-specific products.

Over the years, Shannon and I had so much fun making up the names for the different lines of

❄ *My board is sold in Japan for 850 USD.*

pretty good **FOR A** *girl*

clothing we were involved with: Prom, Tuesday, Blush, Madison, Bliss...the list went on and on. Our best source of names came from lipstick colors. We would go to the mall and pretend to be shopping for makeup at the Mac counter and memorize all the color names. Our ideas for clothing designs mostly came from vintage clothing and thrift store finds and the functions that we needed on the mountain. For example, our favorite piece was a retro coat with sports stripes down the sleeve and an embroidered butterfly on the chest, but it was made of Gore-Tex waterproof fabric.

Back then, as women, we not only had to push our way into the industry side of things, we also had to make sure we were represented in all competitions and getting equal prize money. We were at the top of our sport, but we still knew what it was like to be a female athlete in a male-dominated industry. There were way more guy pros than female pros. If we didn't push it, then everything might be lost for new girl riders out on the mountain, and snowboarding for girls might end up like so many other sports in terms of competitions with no women's divisions, no prize money, no place to even test one another's abilities. So we pushed hard to make sure we represented in every aspect.

At the Air & Style Big Air contest in Innsbruck, Austria, in 1994 there still wasn't even a women's division, even though the event had been around for three years. My brother was entered in the contest and Shannon and I were out there at the practice session checking out the jump because we thought we might be able to do it. The officials came right over to us and said in broken English, "No girls allowed." Oh, sure. Now we were really going to do it. We went back to the car and grabbed our snowboards and started hiking up to the jump. We talked the officials into allowing us three practice jumps and then judging if we were "unsafe." I felt like I was at Boreal trying out for my blue badge. Even though we both crashed hard on our first jump and I knew I'd be paying for it the next day with a stiff neck, there was no way that I wasn't going to do it. By the third try, we passed their test and that night, under the spotlights of the event stadium, in our pink Prom snowboard outfits and hair in pigtails, we jumped the 60-foot gap jump in front of 15,000 people. The announcer kept saying over the loudspeaker, "Those crazy American girls! Those crazy American girls!" But the only thing "crazy" would have been if we had let the opportunity slip by. We weren't able to be "judged" officially because there was only a guys division, so we were the "exhibitionists"—the warm-up clowns

❋ *Designs for my pro model snowboards.*

for that night's circus. But magazine articles later reported that we'd gone bigger than some of the guys that night and probably would have placed in the top ten. It was perfect.

Around this time, I distinctly remember feeling the change in how I was viewed as a female athlete. People around the world were noticing my talents, and for the first time I started hearing the compliment "You're pretty good," not just "You're pretty good for a girl." Maybe it was because I'd been consistently placing well in the halfpipe, or because I had just made a strong statement by jumping a huge big-air jump in Europe, which nobody expected any girl to do. Or, it could have come from newfound respect for crashing so seriously (I definitely had my share of yard sales, losing my goggles, gloves, and hat) after trying to land a cliff and coming back for more. No matter what the exact source was, hearing that and believing that I was pretty good kick-started my drive to be even better, maybe even better than some of the guys. It was happening and I could feel it inside. I was making my mark.

So were other women athletes. Suddenly more companies were launching women-specific equipment and adding women's apparel to their lineup. In the media, magazines were giving girls more coverage. In 1994, I got my first cover (on the back) of the Japanese magazine *Snow Style* with a feature article titled "No Need to Look Like a Guy Anymore." It was my first printed global exposure. In surfing a year later, four-time World Champion Lisa Anderson was on the cover of *Surfer* magazine with a tagline that read "Lisa Anderson Surfs Better Than You." Skateboarder Cara-Beth Burnside was getting feature articles written about her in *Skateboarding* magazine and was the first female to grace the cover of *Thrasher*, a totally core, guy-oriented street skateboard magazine.

A pioneering magazine launched in 1995 called *W.i.G. Magazine*—for Women in General—was the first to showcase the lifestyles of women in action sports like snowboarding, surfing, and skateboarding. The editor

※ *My first magazine cover,*
SnowStyle, *Japan, 1995.*

and publisher was my friend Kathleen Gasperini and the art director was
Dawn Kish, the first woman photographer to break into the boys' club of
snowboarding photography. They told the stories of what it was like to live
the lifestyle of women in snowboarding and had stories, art, and photography from professional athletes and women in the industry. In one

issue, Monica Steward, the cofounder of Bonfire snowboard clothing and best friend of professional rider Michele Taggart, who introduced us, wrote a story called "Both Feet on the Ground." It shocked every one of us. While we were feeling invincible and so alive, Monica had a much bigger story to tell—of being twenty-six years old, a snowboarder, and having breast cancer.

In *W.i.G.* she wrote, "I received the news that we have all heard before, but hope never to hear in our own world. We have seen it on TV, in *Cosmo*, and heard about friends and close and distant relatives who have been diagnosed with breast cancer. We have been told about the monthly exams we are supposed to do to ourselves, but rarely do. At 26, I felt a lump in my breast. I went to the doctor, but he told me it was nothing. He told me what I wanted to hear. I did not pursue getting a mammogram. Why should I? A 26-year-old healthy woman does not get breast cancer. I didn't think so anyway. But three years later, that lump turned out to be 'something.' It was cancer."

Monica went on to talk about her mastectomy, recovering from being severely ill, and about how easy it is to drift into a doom state when you're sick and dealing with moments of terror about your life. She talked about the energy it takes to keep positive in order to heal and acquiring inner strength no matter what's thrown your way and having the strength to catch it in both hands, standing on both feet, with the capability to understand how to deal with it. And she challenged us all by asking, "Why do we need to have a near-death experience to thrust us into living life the way we're supposed to? Every day I get out of bed, set my feet on the floor, and start the day. Have you ever done the same? Ever set your feet on the floor and thought

to yourself how wonderful it is to *have* feet? Feet that have no pain and do exactly what you tell them? We never realize how good something is until it's in pain...or gone."

That story stopped me in my tracks. I thought breast cancer was something that our grandmothers were dealing with. Not us. And not a dear friend fighting for her life and having a mastectomy. There was a trade show coming up in a month and Kathleen, Dawn, Shannon, Lisa, and I planned on getting together with Monica to see what we could do. Her cancer was in remission and at the show, Monica told us how alienated she felt when she was so sick and being diagnosed so young. There was nowhere for her to turn. There were no support groups for people like her and her husband, John, and there was very little research about young women and breast cancer. But she didn't let this get her down. She said she wanted to do something.

We decided to have a snowboarding event like a Lollapalooza on the snow with bands playing and professional snowboarders in a big-air and halfpipe competition. We thought if we could attract people with a fun atmosphere, we could also teach them about breast cancer, or at least make them aware, and maybe show them how to do a self breast exam. Maybe we could also raise a little money and give it to breast cancer research or counseling for young couples dealing with the disease.

Fall turned to winter as we planned our little event over the phone, figuring out the location, where to get a stage, how to sell tickets, and setting the date. We decided on having it at the end of the season, in April, when snowboarding competitions were over, as a last big fun event. Sierra-at-Tahoe resort in northern California stepped up and general manager John Rice said they'd donate ski lift ticket sales to our cause and that their mountain employees would volunteer to help. They said they'd get the word out about our event on local radio and TV stations in Tahoe. Monica and Lisa started calling snowboarding manufacturers to donate clothing, equipment, and gear for auctioning off at the event, and Kathleen and Dawn put together artwork for banners, located stage equipment, volunteers, and contacted the press about the event. Monica decided to call our event Boarding for Breast Cancer, which we hoped would attract snowboarders. Michele Taggart, Shannon, Michael, and I called all our friends and told them that they had to come to our event and represent. No one questioned it. Of course they would come, even though our "prize money" for best snowboarder was donations such as mountain bikes, surfboards, and jackets.

In December, Monica called Kathleen and said she was sick again. The cancer was back inside and she might not be able to make it. We had no idea the extent of her illness. On January 8, 1996, at the age of twenty-nine, she died. It was only three months before our inaugural event.

We were silenced. At Monica's memorial service, which was packed with friends from the snowboarding industry, they talked about Monica's

The Beastie Boys play at the first Boarding for Breast Cancer Snowboard and Music Festival at Sierra-at-Tahoe, California, 1996.

fund-raising event and everyone rallied around the cause. In memory of Monica, we decided to keep going and focused on making it happen. We were able to book bands like M.I.R.V., Tilt, Spent Idols, and Sick of It All to come play. Fifty manufacturers from the snowboarding industry donated product, and John Logic, a former DJ and the owner of a Seattle-based snowboard shop called the Snowboard Connection, volunteered to come down and run our auction. Between myself, Michael, Shannon, and Michele, we had 120 professional riders confirmed to come and throw down their best moves in the halfpipe and big air.

But of all the snowboarders I knew, it was Adam Yauch who could really take our event to the next level. I knew he was a real snowboarder and would be into supporting the cause if he could make it. I called and talked to him and he said OK, they'd be there, but he wanted to play a warm-up show in Tahoe the night before. He recommended we rent out a pizza joint, and I called around and couldn't come up with any. So I called Shaun Palmer, a pro snowboarder who lives in Tahoe, to see if they could play at his house. It turned out he didn't live at the house anymore, but I asked the guy who answered the phone if it was OK if the Beastie Boys played in his living room for a little bit. He quickly said that'd be fine.

The night before the event, we all drove up to Shaun's old house and there was a mile of cars leading down the road to the highway. Obviously word traveled fast. About five hundred people had turned up. We had to push the couches over like barricades. People were just hanging out the windows and in every corner of that house. I made an announcement on the microphone inviting everyone to come to our event the following day and then introduced the Beastie Boys. They came in, set up, and rocked the house.

The next day, April 13, the day of our first Boarding for Breast Cancer Snowboard + Music Festival, all of us girls were there at 5 A.M., looking out over the scene where our stage was set up in the snow, our banners hung along the halfpipe, and the snowboard manufacturer booths and breast cancer awareness education area and art exhibits were all set up. It was quiet and empty but looked like it'd be a sunny day. We were thinking that if we could get five hundred people to show up, we'd raise $4,000 to $5,000 and that'd be pretty good.

That day, 5,600 people showed up. We couldn't believe it. We had the top pro riders in the country like Michele, Shannon, Michael, Barrett Christy, Tricia Burns, Megan Pischki, Bobby Meeks, Shaun Palmer, Jennie Waara, and Athena who came to compete. We all rode hard, putting on a show for this crowd and doing what we knew best to support the cause.

With the Beasties after the show.

Michele Taggart threw down a backside indy 360 into a "boob-grab"—where she literally grabbed her boobs before landing. Shaun caught such big air off the big-air jump people were blown away and photographers couldn't take enough pictures because he was sporting our bright pink ribbons that we passed out to riders to show support. Jennie pulled a 180-method that won her top female status and a Trek mountain bike. Of course, being the creative types that they are, snowboarders made up countless other names for our event other than Boarding for Breast Cancer, like Jibbing for Jugs and BoobAID. Well, as long as it raised awareness...

Back at the stage, John Logic and Lisa tirelessly auctioned off goods all day long, including a scholarship to the Wild Women's Snowboard Camp, boards, boots, clothing, goggles, sunglasses, hats....Snowboarders were everywhere, checking out our art area where we displayed snowboarders' art and photos, the education area where we had jelly boobs we'd gotten from the American Cancer Society that had lumps in them so people could feel what a lump really felt like. In between the Spent Idols set and M.I.R.V., Andrea Martin, the founder of the Breast Cancer Fund, got onstage to remind everyone about the reason for our event: that more than 1.8 million women in this country have the disease and that 1 million more don't know they have it. "It has become an epidemic," she said. "Take charge of your own health, raise money, awareness, and shake things up, shake the tree!"

By the time Sick of It All came on, it was late afternoon and warm and the snow had gone slushy. Everyone had a smile on their tanned faces and you could smell the mix of sweat, wet clothing, and sunscreen in the mosh pit in front of the stage. The music whipped the crowd into a frenzy. Next up were the Beastie Boys. It was so exciting hanging out on the stage with my "event cofounders." Wearing fluorescent orange overalls and looking a lot like Devo, the "Boys" came out and played their own punk performance under the pseudonym of "Quasar." People were going crazy. The moshing got super heavy, which made the snow melt even more and the stage started to sink in the front. "Quasar" kept playing while our boyfriends, also known as our volunteer security guards that day, got sucked into the mosh pit trying to tame the crowd. It was useless, so we all just kept dancing on the stage.

Unfortunately, a rumor had started among the some of the mountain operators who had radios and it was translated back in town by

Wearing Day-Glo
for my Kemper
team photo shoot
at Snowbird,
Utah, 1989.

The lineup of
my boards
over the years.

"Holding On," watercolor, 1999.

Absorbing all that Alaska has to offer, 2002.

Utah powder—
the goods.

Wall ride in
Utah, 1999.

Inverted 360, backcountry Utah, 1998.

Julius and me on our snowboarding adventure.

On the Sims photo shoot in New Zealand, 1995.

Fine Womens Snowboarding Apparel

Designed by Shannon Dunn, Tina Basich, and Swag

/swag • 5651 palmer way, ste. j, carlsbad, ca 92008 send $2 for stickers and info

My first trip
to the snow,
Lake Tahoe,
California.

Warming up for my harp performance.

All girl with a pink bow taped on my head.

During my early softball career.

Self-portrait,
age four.

The industry girls at the SIA trade show in Las Vegas.

Backstage at the Pantera/Black Sabbath concert with John McEnroe, Metallica's Lars Ulrich, Black Sabbath's Tony Iommi, and Dave Grohl.

police who were listening to the channels that "there was a riot up at Sierra." Suddenly we could hear the *whomf, whomf, whomf* of a helicopter's rotor blades overhead, just as Quasar figured out they'd better stop playing or else the stage was going to sink into the moshers. A big voice overhead called out on a megaphone, "Please clear the area, please clear the area..."

Quasar had stopped, but an impromptu skim pool competition, where snowboarders try to skim on their boards at high speed over a pond of melted snow, was already in high gear. One at a time, they came flying down the hill to see how far they could skim before crashing. A snowball fight started on either side of the skim pond, so the heli made another flyby. Of course, people started trying to peg the heli with snowballs. It was insane. Only after getting dunked in icy water, hit in the face with a slush ball, or threatened by another heli flyby, did people start to disperse.

All that was left was lots of garbage, banners askew, roadies packing equipment, and us. We'd forgotten to hire a clean-up crew. So, we grabbed some bags and started packing trash. We were tired but had raised $50,000 and were incredibly happy, talking and laughing about our event as we picked up programs and cups. We knew Monica would have appreciated the whole craziness of it all. That day at least, we knew we were appreciating life, and living the way we were supposed to.

❄ *Backside 360 in*
  the backcountry of Utah.

the birth of
freeriding

Now that there were more established female athletes, representing in contests, doing good things for good causes, we
started to look at what else we really wanted to gain from snowboarding. For me, that answer came on one of the European World Cup tour
events the season of that first Boarding for Breast Cancer. Shannon, my
brother, and I traveled to a competition in this small village in Italy that
was hosting the World Championships. The mountain runs were a total of
700 vertical feet, which is considered very short and small by any standards. There wasn't even enough pitch in the mountain for the racers to
get real speed to make a decent turn in the Giant Slalom course. The
halfpipe was made up with what little snow they had left and was fenced
in so the cows wouldn't walk onto the course. And this course was going
to determine the World Champion! Whatever. We weren't the only ones who
were bummed. All sorts of pros turned up and were disappointed at the

conditions and the location that was chosen by the tour. I looked at the poor condition of the halfpipe and wondered how the weather was in Utah—they probably had fresh powder. Competing on the World Cup was so unglamorous sometimes. Shannon and I knew there was so much more to snowboarding than just competing, like freeriding down a big mountain with fresh powder on it.

We decided to finish up the trip with a freeriding day in Cortina, Italy, which was only an hour away. Cortina has huge mountains and it's where the James Bond movies are filmed because of its scenery. Shannon and I took the gondola up to the very top. We scouted out a run that was untracked powder. We had to traverse on our boards around this cliff range to get to it. We kept going around the mountain and at one point I looked up and thought, "Oh my God!" I told Shannon to stop and look up. We couldn't believe the mountain and this cliff we were standing under—it was about 600 feet above us and we were right underneath it so the view was breathtaking. Down below looked like the perfect run. Wide, open, diamonds of powder. We thought, let's do this run together—we'll do doubles instead of going down one at a time. We dropped in and it was one of the most memorable runs of my life. Fresh powder turns that were perfect, snow flying in plumes with each turn, and we were yelling to each other the whole way down. At the bottom, we high-fived and hugged each other and were crying. We were so wrapped up in this feeling of a powder day in a beautiful place with friends. It was incredibly emotional.

After that experience, it was hard for me to go back on the World Cup because it had changed my views on contests. I couldn't go back to a crappy little 700-foot mountain with an icy halfpipe with flat landings when I could have this. I was getting tired of the grinding schedule of contests. They were so organized, and snowboarding to me wasn't about being organized and having to snowboard in an unsafe halfpipe with flat landings if that's all the mountain provided for the contest. I'd traveled so far from Utah to compete in far from perfect conditions only to hear

over the phone when I checked in with friends at home that I'd "just missed the most incredible snowstorm and fresh powder runs!" I was jealous. "Well, you guys just missed a really 'fun' competition in an icy, bumpy halfpipe on a mountain with no snow." I was traveling in Europe but wondered if it was worth it.

Maybe the other reason I was over the halfpipe was my first-place finishes were getting harder to come by. The level of riding the pipe among the new crop of girls was increasing and the competition was getting tougher. People were specializing in the pipe now and I was not into riding day-in and day-out pipe training. I had to explore the rest of the mountain, ride through the trees, check out natural chutes. My results started to feel the effects—thirds, fourths, fifths . . . I knew I could focus on pipe and train harder and blow off the powder, but I didn't want to. That feeling in Cortina was something special—it was the ultimate snowboarding experience for me. It was real. So, from then on, I decided to stop competing in the halfpipe full time.

I decided I was going to reinvent my riding. Other riders like Dave Downing and Victoria Jealouse never competed anymore, but were sponsored and popular because of the things they'd accomplished in the backcountry or riding big mountains, which was captured on film. Riders like them didn't compete on the World Cup and deal with bad halfpipes. Maybe I could maintain my sponsorship by freeriding like they did? So I announced my decision to sponsors and everyone else that I was done competing in the halfpipe and moving on.

This ended up being a huge mistake.

hotel workout

✳ Shannon Dunn and I have traveled so much on the road together, we've figured out a few great hotel workout travel tips. If you don't like to go downstairs to use the gym, or if your hotel doesn't have a gym, we have some funny techniques for working out in your room.

1. Use the chair in your room to do dips with your butt off the end of the chair.

2. Do regular push-ups against the bed with your upper body on the bed, your feet on the ground.

3. Find some room on the floor to do three sets of sit-ups. I sometimes do them on the bed because

there isn't enough room with all of our luggage and snowboards everywhere. Still, even if you're on the bed, you have to keep your back straight and contract your abdominal muscles to do the most effective sit-ups. These are great to do during commercials if you're watching a movie.

4. Put the phone books and the bible in a pillowcase and use this as a weight to do arm curls or arm lifts off the bed.

5. A stretching and strengthening exercise for your ankles is to stand on one foot on the bed and hold your balance for about a minute. Do this at least three times on each foot. This also helps with your balance. Try it with your eyes closed.

6. If your hotel provides a bathrobe, use the waist tie for stretching out your calves. This is so great after those snowboarding days at resorts that have plenty of toeside traverses. Lie on your back on the bed with one leg extended straight up in the air, wrap the middle of the belt around the ball of your foot, and pull down gently until you feel the stretch.

7. And of course jumping jacks on the bed, because it feels like a trampoline and it's fun. ✳

*First place, Big
Air, at the Winter
X Games, 1998.*

backside 720

As a professional athlete, you cannot simply say you're going to change and expect everyone to go with it. When I announced that I was stopping with halfpipe competitions, my sponsors called immediately and wanted to meet right away, friends called to ask why I was "giving up snowboarding," and the media announced I'd retired.

I hadn't "retired" and I wasn't giving up snowboarding and I hoped my sponsors wouldn't drop me. I'd just stopped competing in the halfpipe. I was transitioning! People do this. Madonna did it a million times, J-Lo, Britney Spears...But I wasn't them and I didn't have millions of dollars from a record label for financial backing. It was too much of a stretch for most people and I wished I'd transitioned more quietly, testing the waters, slowly moving from halfpipe to freeriding and doing more filming on my own. The other problem was that transitioning into becoming a freeriding snowboarding film star was much harder than I imagined. First off, there weren't many girls at Victoria Jealouse's level who were sponsored and didn't compete. The guys who filmed were used to filming with their own group of riders—people they knew who could hit their mark. If I was invited it was often on a fluke because someone had dropped out, and I wasn't prepared to ride on cue all the time because I took too long checking out the jumps or cliffs. It was frustrating, especially when I didn't nail the landings and my segment ended up on the cutting room floor. Sometimes I felt like I was wasting their film and I'm sure they felt that way, too, because I didn't get invited back often.

Filmmaker Justin Hostynek from Absinthe Films was one of the few guys who had the patience to let me figure things out and encourage me, which is why I ended up filming with him from then on. He thought the transition to freeriding idea was a good one for me because he thought I had more talent in freeriding than the pipe anyway. Overall though, filming as a freerider was not enough and I wanted to be part of something bigger. So I had to come up with a Plan B.

Don Bostick, who used to manage GoSkate when I was growing up, first told me about the X Games. He was working for ESPN on the event and he said I should definitely check this out. The X Games were a new concept of having multiple action sports and athletes together in one competition venue. Events like ice climbing, downhill mountain bike racing, shovel racing, snowmobiling, freecross skiing, slopestyle, and snowboarding were all a part of it. There was also a new racing component for snowboarders called boardercross, which included six riders going down the mountain in an elimination format on a course made up of banked turns and whoop-de-dos, which was inspired by how motorcross riders raced on a dirt course. The X Games also offered snowboarders another new event called the big air, which was a single jump off a large ramp where snowboarders performed one freestyle trick in the air. Up until this point, jumps like this in competition were usually in events called obstacle course or slopestyle, which offered medium-sized jumps within a sequence of obstacles like rails or kickers in the snow that each rider had the option to hit while going down a run.

The X Games had combined all of these events over the course of five days and put together an enormous awards ceremony, which they said would be televised around the world. The event also included nightly parties and interviews of athletes throughout the week. It was new and exciting for all of us, because we had never had such potential global recognition. Of course my sponsors encouraged me to enter because, obviously, freeriding was only giving me a little exposure and I'd dropped off

First big-air contest at the Winter X Games, Snow Summit, California, 1997.

the halfpipe scene. I thought it was a good idea, too. The X Games seemed like our version of the Olympics and the events would be telecast to 110 million viewers. With an event like the big air, which I thought I could probably do quite well in, I decided I wanted to be a part of it.

There was something about a big-air event at the X Games that rang true for me. I knew I could do it because I liked catching big air off of cliffs in the backcountry, and while I wasn't getting a lot of film exposure yet, I did have a lot of still shots in magazines from some of my backcountry big airs. I was known for going for it. And with my sponsors and peers thinking I'd retired, it gave me that burning drive to make this *my* new thing and be the best. I had no idea at the time that this transition into big air with the X Games meant I was about to come into a new fame I could never have imagined even on the World Cup tour in Japan. Big air would become what I was most known for in my entire snowboarding career.

While the world was watching the first Winter X Games in 1996, it was important to have girls represented in every division. All of the female snowboarding professionals believed this. The X Games provided the perfect transition for many of my friends and we all signed up for different kinds of events. Leslee Olson, known for her giant slalom racing, entered in boardercross. Tara Dakides did halfpipe and slopestyle—the latter of which she dominated. And for me this was a perfect transition from my halfpipe and filming into big air.

Sixteen girls entered the big-air contest that year, but when it came down to the day of competition, only four of us showed up that morning to get our bibs. We'd been scoping the jump ahead of time and even the guys were scared. It was risky and dangerous—a 50-foot jump with snow conditions that were icy and firm, which meant the speed up to the lip of the launch would be really fast, which meant the air would be big, and the landing would be harder to control. It was completely sketchy, to say the least, and scared off most of the competitive field. Barrett Christy, April Lawyer, Tara Zwink, and I were the only girls who committed to doing it in the end. Of course, we couldn't back out because we had to have a girls division. But looking at that big air was scary beyond belief because it was so much bigger than any jump I'd ever hit before. Not to mention the fact that this would be in front a huge audience and televised so there was that pressure of it being a "comeback moment" even though I'd never really gone anywhere. The other girls looked at me like I looked at them—if one of us didn't do it, it was doubtful there'd be a girls division in the future. We had to make sure this happened at the X Games.

Up at the starting gate, it was a different scene than at the pipe because there were only four of us entered. It reminded me of my first contest at Donner Ski Ranch, when there were only four girls that I knew who even snowboarded. I think the guys thought we were going to back out. They were checking to see the fear in our eyes, which we had, I admit. But we didn't back out. All of us found our confidence and took our runs, even though we were extremely nervous. I did a backside 360, my best trick at the time, and ended up third behind Barrett and Tara. It wasn't anything spectacular, but it was one of those days when I was glad to get through it and at the same time was so proud of having been a part of the first big air in the Winter X Games.

The X Games gave me a new focus, and like other riders, I knew this meant our sport was getting the attention it deserved. Of course I wanted to be a big player in all of this because I'd worked so hard and this was my life. From that point on, I'd freeride and film with Justin to *gradually* work my way into that backcountry film scene, but did it in between big-air contests. I felt good. The next summer, I spent almost every day riding the glacier at Mt. Hood High Cascade Snowboard Camp, a place where snowboarders go to ride in the off-season to train for big air. I was hucking myself over and over off jumps to try to improve my rotations. While sometimes you have to just throw down the motions and see what your body and talents are capable of doing, I'd learned doing well also came from having the right mind-set. I'd been pulling off my backside 360s in a few competitions, which my body was now so programmed to do, and was ready to push it to the next level. I knew there had to be a way to pull off two rotations in midair—a backside 720—and was determined to learn it. Only, no one had ever seen a girl do it before, so if I could pull this off at a big-air contest, I was sure to win.

Ask Tony Hawk about his 900 skateboarding trick. It took him years and hundreds of crashes to finally land it. People didn't think it was possible because no one had ever seen it done before. Snowboarders didn't even know if a backside 720 was possible at one time. I remembered back at my first World Championships when I was so impressed by Amy Howitt, who had gotten one foot in the air out of the halfpipe, and it made me leave that competition wanting to be as good as her. And now I had a much bigger goal: a backside 720 over a 60-foot jump.

I tried to go faster down the ramp, spin tighter, but just kept crashing, over and over again, trying to figure it out. I had bruises all over my body from crashing and needed to get it into my head that it was possible and actually *see* or visualize myself completing the trick. Ironically, the importance of visualization was something I had learned from drag car racing school in California at the Pomona Raceway the previous year. I'd been invited to take the drag car racing course for a TV show that featured female athletes doing crazy stunts. There were three of us "crazy athletes"—a professional surfer, a Tai Kwan Do champion, and me. We walked into driving school for the eight-hour class before racing and it was filled with musclehead, hot-rod guys who stared at us with that old familiar look like, "What are these *girls* doing here?" But we all completed the two-day course and clocked in some of the fastest quarter-mile drag times at 155 mph in our $120,000 race car rentals. Although some of the guys didn't like getting beaten by a girl (so what's new), we made an impression, I'm sure.

What I gained most, however, was a new view on the importance of real-time visualization that can be applied to all sports, whether you're drag car racing or doing a jump on a snowboard. In class, they taught us that you have to visualize the action in real time, at the real speed. Before I'd learned this, I used to visualize the movements my body would have to make, moving in a certain way, practicing throwing my shoulder

❋ *Drag car racing school at the Pomona Raceway.*

over my front leg to do an invert, and then doing that over and over, but had never visualized doing it in real time. So, now I'd visualize taking my three breaths before dropping into the run and then visualize the actual speed of myself coming up to the jump, rolling my shoulder over my front leg, grabbing my board, and then landing and riding down to a stop. By visualizing this in real time, you're not skipping any part of it, because when you drop in and visualize it as you're doing it, you're prepared for the whole thing, including landing and riding away from it, so nothing can catch you off guard.

With the power of visualization, it still took maybe another twenty times of trying my 720, almost rotating enough, then crashing, before it suddenly clicked. One time, I almost landed it, but from then on, I could feel what it would be like and I knew it was possible now. I knew I could do it.

However, doing it in competition was another thing altogether.

By January 1998, at the time of the Winter X Games big-air snowboarding competition, launching over 60-foot gap jumps on my snowboard was considered one of my specialties. I'd placed top three many times in smaller competitions and often took large jumps in the backcountry for filming. I felt comfortable in the air and I liked the feeling of flying.

Still, I was nervous. I wanted to win so badly with my new trick that it just burned in my stomach. I wanted that recognition, like when people noticed I could throw a ball really hard, or when I'd throw down new tricks in the halfpipe on the World Cup tour. It was a competitive drive, but not so much because I wanted to beat the next girl. I wanted to be recognized for pushing the level of the sport to something no one had ever imagined, like a freestyler winning a slalom race with a Domino's pizza box wrapped around her arm. I knew no one else had pulled this trick before in a big-air competition and I wanted this moment to be mine.

I woke up at 7 A.M. and checked the weather as usual. It was sunny. It's so much easier to perform your best when you can actually see the landing. Snowy competition days are tough because visibility sucks of course, and because conditions are constantly changing, including wind factor and the speed of the snow. If the snow is hard or cold, the speed of the snow means you go faster. If it's warm and slushy, the snow is slower and you have to get more speed to clear the jump. In bad weather, snow conditions can change in minutes and the last thing you want to do is misjudge the speed you need to clear the jump, launch off the lip too slow, dangling there, or get pulled by the wind in midair. It can mean the difference between first and last place, or lead to serious injury. I was never as worried about the placing as I was about the serious risk of getting injured. It's not just in Alaska where the weather matters to snowboarders; all snowboard contests can be cancelled due to weather.

That morning I stayed in my pj's for a good twenty minutes watching the Weather Channel and stretching with a couple of yoga moves. I never eat on competition days, which is probably the worst thing I can do for my energy level, but I can't handle having a nervous stomach full of food. I packed my backpack with extra goggles and my CD player and headed up to the mountain.

We usually get about an hour of practice time to warm up on the jump before the competition begins. First things first: I checked out the jump. My best place for visualizing is standing right on top of the jump. I have to talk myself into it every single time. You'd think by this point I might be over this feeling. But I'm not. I always watch a couple of people hit the jump before I go. I'm a visual person. I watch where they start from, speed checks, and how the jump throws them. Most of all, I watch how hard the landing looks. I watch because I can learn from whatever mistakes they make by misjudging things—even slightly. No one ever wants to be the first to hit the jump. Sometimes a team manager will use a radio to let everyone at the top know how much speed to take to clear the landing. But there wasn't a team manager at the bottom at this event, so I had to make my own judgment call.

OK, I thought to myself, it's now or never. I didn't want my first jump to be during competition so I decided to take the practice jumps. I grabbed my board and my helmet and hiked up to the start gate. I had Metallica playing on my CD player. I don't ride with a player anymore, but when all you're doing is hiking along the side of the jump to the start gate, it helps to listen to music instead of your own heavy breathing. Plus, it gets me in the right mood to huck over a 60-foot jump. That first jump is always the hardest part for me. How fast should I go? Did I used the right wax on my board, which can mean the difference between going too fast or too slow? Is the snow going to be fast today?

I did a straight jump first—leaving the jump facing forward and landing forward—to be on the safe side. I worked my way up, pulling more difficult tricks, to prepare for what I knew I had to do for my competition jump—a backside 720. After all the time practicing at Mt. Hood on the glacier, I'd tried this trick only once before at a big-air competition, two months earlier in Aspen, Colorado. I'd gotten my spin around, but didn't stick the landing. Still, it'd made an impression. There was a buzz about it among my peers. People saw that it could happen—that a female professional snowboarder might be able to pull off a backside 720 in competition.

I had to be the first.

Each competitor got three jumps and the score of the best two jumps combined would win. The adrenaline was flowing in each of us, but compared with other competitive sports, like gymnastics, where the girls

barely talk to one another, the scene was supportive and exciting. Everyone was cheering each other on. I couldn't do what I do if the other girls
were trying to psych me out. It helped me to not be so hard on myself
and stay focused on landing my trick. Win or lose, it would be an incredible experience because millions of people would see girls snowboarding
and understand that another whole level was possible.

I had to try my backside 720 right then. On my first jump of the
competition, I'd decided to go for it. The official called my name. A few
of my friends knew what I was going to try and gave me that look like

*Practicing at
Mt. Hood, Oregon.*

"You can do it" in the starting gate. It was my turn—this was it. My heart started pounding as I strapped my board on my feet and entered the starting gate. I tightened my goggles and ratcheted down my bindings a little tighter, looking down at the jump. I could see the crowds of people around the landing zone with hats on like colorful dots in a painting. I had to block them out and visualize what I knew I could do. I took three deep breaths and dropped onto the runway. In my head I repeated the words "strong legs, strong legs..." The speed was fast and I launched off the jump, twisted my body to begin the rotation, spun around once very tight and fast, then went for another spin in the air. I think I actually closed my eyes for part of the trick. I came around to see my landing and my rotation was perfect, square to the mountain. I landed exactly where I had visualized it. I could not believe it. I could barely breathe. I had done it! I surprised myself. I surprised people watching. Performing a backside 720 over a 60-foot gap jump was no longer impossible. No one would dare say *that* was pretty good for a girl! I could hear all my snowboard friends up at the starting gate cheering for me. It was one of the greatest moments of my snowboarding career. My next two jumps included one more 720 and a 360, which, combined, were good enough for first place. I had just won my first gold medal at the ESPN X Games and thousands of people had suddenly seen me at my best. Interestingly, even a few pro snowboarder guys came up to me after that contest and told me they couldn't yet do that trick. They looked at me a little differently— they were truly impressed. It was such an amazing feeling.

1998 Summer
X Games.

rockstar

By now, female athlete–endorsed snowboards and apparel were the norm. I had my own signature snowboard boot from Airwalk, apparel line from Tuesday, and Tina Basich snowboard model by Sims. The year after I did my backside 720, I sold 6,700 pro model snowboards, mostly in Japan, and it was the top-selling pro model for my company— outselling all of the guys. This was my biggest year so far. It was no longer a question of whether women were marketable or not, they definitely had a place in the global snowboarding market. Women in sports were getting more media coverage, and I was now on my fourth cover for a snowboard magazine.

After winning at the X Games, I was starting to feel the pressure to win again at the next contest. Big air was so popular at the X Games that they started including it at the Summer X Games in 1998, not just winter. Summer X Games had events like rock climbing, BMX, skateboarding, motorcross, and now...snowboarding big air. The thing is you have to have snow for a big-air jump, so the X Games built a huge "slope" from a maze of scaffolding with man-made snow on it.

I got on the road in my '62 Impala, ready to roadtrip from my aunt and uncle's house in Los Angeles to San Diego for the event, top down, all summer lovin' feelin'. About an hour south of L.A., I had a blowout and rode on my rims for two miles until I could get across the seven-lane

❄ *My '62.*

highway to pull over. I got out and tried to get the tire off with my socket wrench, but it wasn't the right size because I'd just pimped-out my car with new rims. So I hiked down the highway, off the exit, found a gas station, and they gave me a bigger crowbar that they said would fit my rims. I had to pay them $20 to borrow it for thirty minutes. I went back to my Impala and changed the tire myself and was freaking out because I knew I'd be late for practice and I had a new version of my 720

I wanted to test. When I finally drove into San Diego, from about a mile away I could see the scaffolding of the big-air jump popping out of the city. It was quite an engineering feat and just amazing—so big and so out of place. Like a white-covered roller coaster. I quickly checked in, got my competition bib, and ran to the jump with my gear just in time to hear them cancel the practice session because the heat was melting the snow. They had to blow more snow the rest of the day and all night to have enough for the competition the next day. It was so frustrating. I really needed that practice session.

Anyway, the next day I decided to pull an inverted version of my 720. I'd only practiced it a few times and should have practiced it more before doing it in competition, but it was summer, and I thought I'd try it. I was so excited about having pulled my backside 720 in the winter games that I had this feeling if I tried the invert version and failed, it was OK, sort of, because at least I was pushing it even more and trying a new trick. It got me off the hook if I crashed, I figured, and so I wasn't really nervous.

I was more nervous about hiking the scaffolding with these tiny steps in snowboard boots all the way to the top of the jump. It was weird to look out over this crowd of people in tank tops and shorts, and here we were at the top of a snowboard jump in the summer in San Diego, in snowboard pants and gloves and T-shirts. We were so hot that beads of sweat kept dripping in our goggles. I still wore goggles as a protective eyepiece, but it's strange to be wearing them around in the summer, like in a desert sandstorm or something. I liked the jump even though it was man-made because it was easier to judge my speed, since there was only one place to start from at the starting gate. It wasn't like you had the option of starting higher up the "mountain" or lower. We all started in the same place. And the weather wasn't changing—it was just hot. Plus there was padding on the flat deck, so if you didn't clear the landing, you would just land in the foam. We all talked about that foam, wishing we had it all the time.

When I pulled my inverted 720 that day, I pulled it off just enough to get around and land it, but it wasn't all that graceful and I popped back a bit to catch myself on the landing. However, it was good enough for second place and I was stoked I had another X Games medal. I don't mean to be ungrateful—I was very excited about the medal—but frankly, it was summer and I had that summertime feeling. I really just wanted to get out of snowboard boots and back into my flip-flops and cruise in my Impala.

Over the course of the next year, I started to notice a difference in the pressure I was putting on myself and the expectations of others. I was now the big-air favorite to win or at least place second and that pressure weighed heavily on my mind. I started to feel judged with every jump I took, even in practice. I can tell you that being the underdog and winning is the ultimate high. But winning when you're expected to win is more of a feeling of relief that you can even come out there and pull it off. Somehow it's more satisfying to prove people wrong than to prove them right.

The women's abilities in snowboarding were getting more competitive. Girls like Leslee Olson, Tara Dakides, and Barrett Christy were all raising the bar and pushing the levels of competition in the big-air category. The contests themselves were getting more competitive and had bigger sponsorship dollars. Suddenly the sponsor banners that hung along the side of the halfpipe went from being the local skate shop and ski resort to corporate banners by Taco Bell, AT&T, and Mountain Dew. I remember us all talking about it at the X Games and wondering, "What do they want with us?" I couldn't figure it out. There was a shift in views and it seemed as though, suddenly, the green-haired punk kid on a snowboard who was once not allowed at ski resorts was "marketable" and considered "cool" by mainstream America.

My personal life was changing drastically, too. I hadn't had a boyfriend for a while because I was busy riding year-round, and now I was getting loads of attention from the press. I was busy doing commercials and interviews and even a video game characterization. And then I met Dave Grohl. His band the Foo Fighters played at the third Boarding for Breast Cancer event in Tahoe. It was a mild attraction at first and we only talked a little bit at the event. But two weeks before the Summer X Games in 1998, I met him again at a video game convention in Atlanta. He was there to play at the kick-off Sony party of the video convention and I was there to promote the new snowboarding video game, Pro-Boarder, in which I was featured as a character. There was a strong chem-

Goofing off on the Pocket Rockets with Dave.

istry between us. I blew off practicing for the X Games up at Mt. Hood to go on our first official date: the Tibetan Freedom Concert in Washington, D.C.

This was the beginning of a crazy summer, filled with award shows, goofing off on Pocket Rocket minibikes, touring, and several awkward and unfamiliar situations. I thought I knew what pressure was all about before I met Dave, but I learned quickly from dating someone "famous" that there are pressures you cannot avoid. It made my snowboarding world seem tame and controllable. I was used to being outdoors and traveling to mountains to go snowboarding. My destinations were usually peaceful and calming, with fresh powder. Suddenly I was with a guy who was going from city to city every night and being in clubs and concert halls. We were always up late. And it seemed like everyone wanted a piece of him. I'd be leaving backstage with him, holding hands, and girls would still be coming up and giving him their phone numbers. It was a vibe I was not used to and I tried to be cool with it all.

Over the two years that we dated, snowboarding seemed to take a backseat in my priorities. I was spending more time with Dave and experiencing his lifestyle, which wasn't always easy. One night, Dave was invited to the Playboy mansion for a Midsummer Night's Dream pajama party. The whole band decided to go, so we went shopping for pj's. I bought Pooh Bear flannel pajamas and a stuffed Pooh Bear to carry with me, plus slippers, and I wore my hair in pigtails. I felt like I had the complete outfit. Dave got silk pajamas, which is what all the guys there were wearing, even Hugh. When we got out of the limo at the mansion, the first person I saw was Tori Spelling in like ten-inch spiked heels that could poke an eye out, and she only wore a feather boa and a skimpy teddy. I instantly felt so out of place; it was more like a lingerie party. I should have known. There were boobs and butts and feather boas everywhere—I was definitely the only girl there in flannel.

Like high school, I fell under the pressure of being different, but this time I headed straight for the bar. A few lemon drop shots later, I was making friends with all the bunnies and even got a photo taken with Hugh and Miss June. It ended up being a really fun party with lots of weird celebrity sightings like Jim Carrey, George Clooney, Weird Al Yankovic, and Jerry Springer, who told me to never watch his show because it was trash. By the end of the night I was regretting my decision to drink my insecurities away and ended up puking on the front yard while we were waiting for the limo to take us home. I was so embarrassed. I remember getting in the limo and yelling back to the group of people standing there, "Please tell Hugh I'm sorry for puking in his front yard!"

Even with all of these new experiences, at this point, my career was stronger than it had ever been and I was getting lots of attention for pulling off my 720 and doing an inverted version at the X Games. The film guys who didn't want to use me before were suddenly calling. Guess I wasn't a waste of film anymore. But I stuck with Justin because he'd stuck it out with me. Yet even with all of this new fame, there was also an invitation to be a part of Dave's life and I was falling for him. In some weird way, I found myself falling in love with Dave and out of love with snowboarding. My priorities were changing and this fueled my fears and the pressures to still compete.

I was entered in the big air for the 1999 Winter X Games and anxiously awaiting snowboarding season. As winter approached, I started to have major anxiety about the contest. I was returning to defend my first-place title and felt so much pressure that I would wake myself up in the middle of the night blurting out, "I can't do it!" I didn't know how to handle this new kind of pressure. I had this awful feeling that I was going to get injured at the contest. Maybe a small part of me wanted to be injured with a tiny sprained ankle just so I wouldn't have to do it. It gave me a stomachache just thinking about it.

Still, I was a professional and had obligations to perform, so in January of 1999, I traveled out to the X Games with the intention of competing in the big-air event. I had not shared my feelings of fear with anyone, not even with Dave, who was now my boyfriend. I showed up ready to go, but not really. The big-air event was scheduled for the last day of the contest. I waited through five days of competition and ended up not competing in the slopestyle event to save my energy for the big air.

On the morning of the big-air competition, I woke up and forced myself to go through the motions. I stretched out and made sure my board was waxed and ready to go. I watched the Weather Channel and packed up my backpack as usual. As I was going through my morning routine, I realized that I really wanted out of this situation. The night before, Dave had told me that he wanted to have a family with me, and it was in the forefront of my mind. This was the first time I thought it was for real. As I stood on top of the jump at the big air, staring blankly at the landing, I thought maybe I was ready to give this up and start the next stage of my life. But could I give it up?

Ironically, the weather was changing and the wind was picking up and the contest ended up being postponed until the next day. I thought this was a sign that I wasn't supposed to compete. I was thinking too much and reading into every situation that surfaced. My parents were there and their flights were not changeable and Dave had to get back to start recording his new album, which meant if I did it, I'd be there alone to compete. I decided not to do the contest. There was no way I could compete in this frame of mind. I couldn't even visualize myself at the top of the jump. We all packed up and left town. On our drive to the airport I almost turned around, thinking, "How could I not be a part of this?" Snowboarding was my life. But for some reason I think I wasn't supposed to be in that competition. I was so confused about my place in snowboarding and trying to figure out what my place was in Dave's life, not to mention my own. Things were so unclear and confusing and I needed to figure it all out, but had no idea what to do.

should I let my boyfriend teach me how to snowboard?

✱ Only if he has great patience.
It's easy to get frustrated, so if you don't want to hear
the phrase "Just do it!" all day long, take a lesson and
meet up with him for lunch. The lessons at resorts are
affordable these days and really helpful. Snowboard
instructors have come up with techniques that really
help to make your first day a great experience. Also,
it's a little embarrassing falling on your face all day
in front of your boyfriend, and believe me you will
take some falls. ✱

should I teach my boyfriend how to snowboard?

✱ If you have a great, easygoing
relationship, absolutely! Take the opportunity to tell your
boyfriend what to do for the day. It can be a great day
filled with funny moments and laughs. But, if your
relationship is at all competitive, teaching your boyfriend
how to snowboard could lead you down the wrong path.

In this case, I would recommend putting him in a lesson while you go out and get some fresh powder turns, and meet up with him for lunch.

Most of my boyfriends have been great snowboarders. Trying to keep up with them on the mountain always pushed my abilities and confidence. The days of trying to keep up with Andy Hetzel at Snowbird in Utah made me a better snowboarder. He never let me take the easiest line down the mountain. One of the first questions I asked David when I met him was, "Do you snowboard?" He had a few days under his belt. He did pretty well the few days we went snowboarding together. I always pretended to look the other way when he'd catch an edge and fall. ✸

*Practicing
at the '99
X Games.*

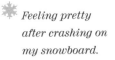 *Feeling pretty after crashing on my snowboard.*

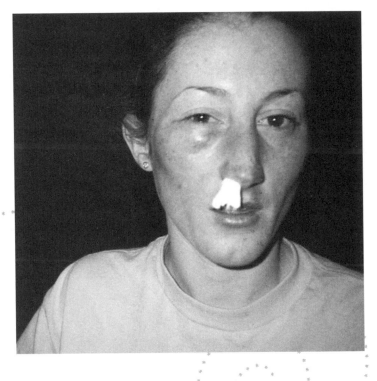

downtime

used to think there wasn't a "zone" required for an athlete to be in to have a peak performance. I thought if you had the balls to do it, then just go out there and do it. But why couldn't I just do it at the X Games? Physically, I knew I was capable of jumping the big air at that contest, but my mind-set was not in the zone. I didn't realize that frame of mind isn't something that's always there.

I had not entered a contest since driving away from the Winter X Games. I thought I'd try the big-air competition again in the Summer X Games. Yet for the rest of the season, I was still snowboarding hard, traveling a lot, and filming with Justin.

On the last day of the season, May 20, 1999, at Mammoth Mountain, California, I was doing an interview for *Transworld Snowboarding* magazine and needed a sequence shot of my backside 720. I had to get this shot to make the interview complete. I was burned out from being on the road and feeling like I wasn't 100 percent that day. Summer was around the corner and I was ready for warm weather and flip-flops. Dave was recording his new album and I was looking forward to spending more time with him. I didn't read my instincts, which basically said I didn't feel like snowboarding that day. My head just wasn't in it. I felt like I was forcing myself to do the photo shoot when I was really just in the mood to have a kick-back last day of the season riding with my girlfriends.

That morning, I was warming up with my backside 3's (360 rotations) off the jump where the photo shoot was to take place in the snowboard park. All morning I'd been looking for the photographer who was supposed to get this shot. I went inside for lunch, then came back out to look for him again. I finally found him, and by the time we were set for the shot, the snow had turned to slush, which meant it was a slower run into the jump than it had been earlier in the day.

I was rushing myself and didn't take that into consideration. I started at the same point I had been in the morning and headed for the jump knowing that I only had to pull this off once and the photographer would get the sequence shot and my obligations would be filled. I was over it, riding that day, competing that season, and wanted to figure out my life.

I thought I had the perfect amount of speed, but when I took off from the lip and launched into the air, in that first second, I knew I was going too slow. I was already in the rotation of my 720, spinning as tightly as I could, wanting to get really small so maybe my spin would make up for my lack of speed. But I didn't even get my spin all the way around. It's a gut-wrenching feeling dangling in the air, just knowing I'm never going to make the landing, let alone the trick. There's a split second when everything's in slow motion. Looking down at the landing zone from the air, I'm thinking, "How much is this going to hurt me?"

I landed flat, on the top deck, all the air knocked from my lungs, missing the downhill slope of the landing by two feet. It all seemed so slow in the air, but it happened really fast. I crashed so hard—like hitting cement—that my body bounced like a rubber doll with a board attached into the landing zone. I just lay there, absolutely motionless.

Another snowboarder who was also filming went off right behind me and almost ran into me because I was just lying there. Photographer Patti Segovia was nearby and ran over to help me take my board off my feet. I don't know why, but I told her my arms were OK and she dragged me by my arms off to the side of the jump.

Usually when I crash I do a flex test where I flex my neck, then my arms, then my back, butt, thighs, calves, feet, checking to see if everything is OK. This time I didn't do that because I could feel immediately all of my energy rushing to the bottom of my right leg. I knew something was hurt, but I'd never broken a bone before so I didn't know what that felt like. I was sitting on the side of the run holding my leg up in the air in case it was swelling inside my boot, replaying what had just happened in my head. My leg didn't hurt, it just felt really hot, and I was in shock. That day, I happened to be snowboarding with a group of girlfriends and they all came down when they saw me crash. They kept saying, "If it was broken you would be screaming right now. You probably just sprained it." I believed them. But they were so wrong.

I got towed down in the emergency sled by ski patrollers. It costs $800 to be driven to the hospital in the ambulance from the resort and they gave me the option to find my own ride, so I called my friend and teammate Mark Frank to come pick me up because my car was parked at the hotel we were all staying at. He drove my Impala up the mountain and took me to the hospital. If you're going to ride to the hospital, you might as well ride in style. I was wheeled into the emergency room by a nurse. She let go of the wheelchair for a second to get something and the chair went forward and I instinctually put my leg out to catch myself and put all of my weight on my hurt leg. That's when I felt the pain. It was sharp like a knife twisting in, causing shooting pains up my bones. Tears started rolling down my face.

They put me on so much morphine I was slobbering on myself and called my mom and dad and Dave and left the most pathetic messages. The doctors said they were going to cut off my boot to get to the injury and I said, "No!" I'd worn these boots all season and in snowboarding, having a pair of boots that are perfectly worn to your foot is a valuable thing. I didn't want them to cut it off, so I took it off myself and forced my foot out of my boot. When they took my sock off, my foot looked disgusting, it was so swollen. It didn't look like a foot—it was all crooked. It was already starting to turn yellow and blue. I was dazed staring at it and kept saying in my head, "That's not my foot, that's not my foot..." It was the only way I could remove it from my body because having a part of your body broken like that makes you sick to your stomach. I felt like I was going to faint.

They took X rays and came out and told me the details of my injury. I had a broken fibula and tibula with a spiral fracture up one side. I didn't understand the extent of my injuries and stared at my doctor. What was he saying? Things kept echoing. Did he just say I was not going to be snowboarding for a while? How long? A month? All season?? But I'm a professional athlete! This is my life. It is my career. I cannot be hurt. I cannot not snowboard. What about my sponsors?

This was the first time that I was forced to take time off from snowboarding without my making that decision. It was so unfair. I'd trained so hard. My parents drove from Sacramento straight to the hospital to be with me. The hospital flew in a doctor from L.A. and I was operated on the next day. He put three pins in my ankle and it looked like a Frankenstein attachment with stitches going up both sides of my leg.

I spent the next month at my parents' house, living in the recliner chair in the living room. My mom bought me so many art supplies to keep me busy, and I think I watched every single movie from Block-

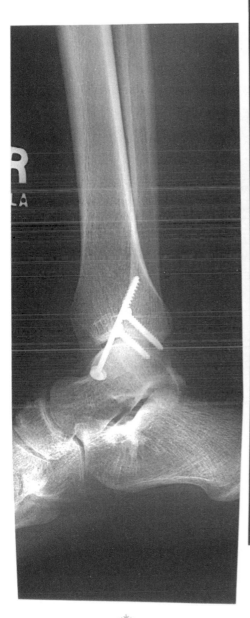

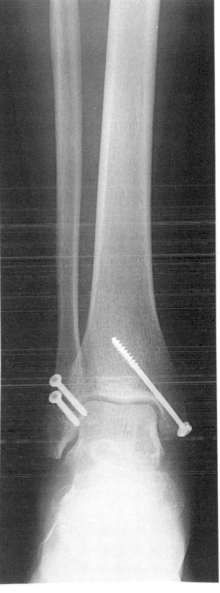

✳ *My hardware.*

buster. It was so hard for me to get around with crutches and it started messing with the alignment of my back so I ended up not using them. I would literally scoot around the house on my butt to avoid using crutches. It was horrible and humbling. I was a big-air snowboarder who'd jumped off cliffs and 60-foot gaps and ridden Alaska's backcountry. Now I was on my butt, not even able to walk. I had so much time to think about everything. I thought about the times when I'd call from Alaska to check in on my friend Angie at home, and she would tell me about her day, her job, being stuck in traffic, going to the gym on the way home, plans for a barbecue and camping trips on the weekends. Some days I'd think, I wish that traffic was my only worry. It sounded so safe and in a weird way I was jealous. My life had no schedule and was dangerous and unpredictable. I'd been riding nonstop, winters and most summers, for twelve years. But I was so used to feeling the seasons and I loved the anticipation of new snow, how it smelled when the seasons changed, and how it felt breathing in the cold air. Now, I was broken down and I couldn't feel the seasons at all. I couldn't feel the snow under my feet.

After being laid up for a month, I was ready for my leg to be better and to get my life back to normal—at least to be able to walk. I thought about what Monica had said, about being fortunate enough to at least be able to put both feet on the ground and appreciate the simple fact that I was living. What I had in comparison was nothing. It's funny how you don't think of such things until they happen to you, and then it's the worst thing in the world and you remember all that you'd thought you'd learned but obviously, maybe, truly didn't absorb.

When I went in for my walking cast, the doctor said he was going to move my foot to a 90-degree angle, but before he even finished the sentence I said, "You can't move it, it's broken." He moved it and I fainted. He had to wake me up with smelling salts. I was pathetic, but this was my first injury and I didn't know what to expect. Up until this moment I had felt completely invincible. I was Superwoman and could do anything on my snowboard. I was in the zone. After I got hurt, I realized how much it really breaks you down. You have so much downtime to really think about the risks you're taking and the consequences that they bring. It's crazy to know that no matter how much I'd trained and practiced, I still didn't have total control of my career. It was a horrible reality check.

Angie taking care of me and painting my nails while I'm laid up in the recliner.

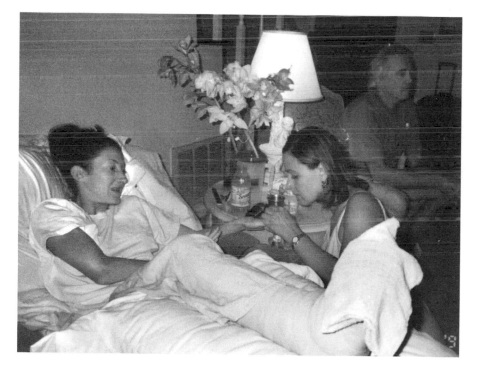

I was also about to turn thirty years old and couldn't help but wonder if this was a turning point in my career. I was now one of the older female professional snowboarders, but those little girls coming into the sport hadn't stepped up and taken me out yet. In the span of my career so far, I'd already seen girls come in and out of the sport for various reasons like lack of sponsorship, bad attitude, or injuries. I still felt like I wanted more out of snowboarding, but wondered if the circumstances I was now in would allow me to continue. I didn't want an injury to be the reason I stopped snowboarding professionally. I had assumed that would be my choice—when I got married and had kids, when I was ready to move on. I was feeling so down and desperately needed to feel something good was happening.

The highlight of my summer was when Lisa Hudson threw my thirtieth birthday party. She rented out the Boom Boom Room, a popular bar in San Francisco known for great live blues music, during the Summer X Games—where I was supposed to be competing in the big air—and got all of my sponsors to pitch in money to throw the party. She had a salsa band play, a photographer taking black-and-white Polaroid photos, and a big birthday cake. Old and new snowboarding photos decorated the walls. It was like walking through a photo gallery of the history of my life. My mom had sent out pages of a book to all of my friends for everyone to draw a picture or write a poem for me. My brother had hand-carved the outside of the book and put it all together.

Dave gave me diamond earrings that night just before the party, wrapped in a blue Tiffany box. I was so surprised. I hadn't worn earrings in years because jewelry got in the way of my snowboarding and all I could think of when I opened the box was, "Oh no, I hope the holes in my ears didn't close." I don't think he even noticed that I'd never worn earrings before. I said I had to get ready and I went to the bathroom and tried so hard to poke them through because I wanted to wear them right then and there. I wanted to feel like everything was all right and all I had to do was get these earrings in. I tried so hard and it hurt because I couldn't get them through and my ears started to bleed and I was already running late . . . so I stopped and cleaned my ears, but they stung the rest of the night.

My broken foot didn't keep me from dancing on the dance floor with my walking cast and my Snoop Doggy Dogg cane. We danced all night. That was the night that Tony Hawk did his famous 900 trick, so he showed up later with all of the skaters who were ready to celebrate. Tony took all of the balloons and tied them to himself and did some break-dancing moves on the dance floor. There was even an Eminem sighting at the bar, which was weird because I doubt he knew it was a birthday party for me. The place was packed and everyone was having a great time. It was so much more than I ever expected. Lisa, my friends, my sponsors, and even ESPN just went over the top. It was so relieving and fun.

I wish I could have kept mainlining my happiness that way, but it had to come from inside, and I knew this. My earlobes hurt and I put the diamonds in the blue Tiffany box back in my luggage until I could get my ears repierced. I put so much time into being with my family and friends, and so when someone comes into my life, I give my time to them. I write to them or call or make sure I'm in contact. I travel so much that it takes time to come back into a friendship. But I work hard at this because friends are so important to me. I was trying to be strong in my relationship with Dave. He was busy recording his new album and I thought I should be there for him and I also struggled to balance my time with my family and friends, plus focus on healing my leg.

My body was naturally healing itself, but my mind was far behind. I had to get back into the mind-set of snowboarding. It was a tough uphill battle, and I didn't even know that it wasn't at its worst yet. To get back to snowboarding, I had to rally my shit together and pull my confidence back up, so that when my leg was healed, my mind knew how to jump again.

It started with a summer full of physical therapy, which is where I learned so much about how my body heals itself. I did really simple exercises and it felt so weird that I couldn't even flex my foot. It seemed like it would take forever to get back to normal and be able to fit comfortably back into my snowboard boot. I wondered if my foot would be as strong as before and if I'd be able to return to my way of riding. I couldn't imagine limiting my snowboarding to just cruising down the easy runs.

I know you can't focus on an injury and there's no way you'll recover if you do, but being hurt, as a professional athlete, shocks you to the

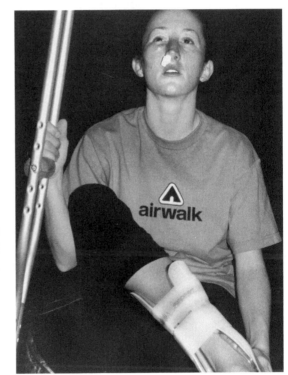

❄ *Sporting my cast and crutches.*

bones. It took more energy than anything I'd ever done before just to keep positive and have the strength to get healthy. The only comfort came when I would think about the fact that my leg was going to recover, which meant I would be snowboarding again soon. Snowboarding was such a big part of my life. It was my identity. It was something that kept me on course and gave me purpose and made me into something that I didn't know I could be. I would never be able to let go—I loved it. I had to get back.

But there was Dave. His life was busy with his own pressures. He had multimillion-dollar record contracts, deadlines with record labels, music videos, press tours, and all along was trying to maintain a focus on being creative and writing music. It was exhausting to me. I don't know how he can do it. The pressure was too much for our relationship to handle. You can only give up so much of your heart and your career and your time and your spirit, and here I was, giving it all up for a guy and losing myself in the process. There has to be a balance or you just simply run out, go on empty. I felt like I was taking time away from his career, which was his priority—totally pulling mine in the backseat without even realizing it. I don't know how anyone in his profession can have a normal relationship with a girlfriend...or two, as it turned out. I found out secondhand, through the grapevine, when it seemed like everyone else in the world knew about it but me. I was so disappointed and pissed at myself for being sucked in. Breakups suck. But Rockstar exits are the worst. All I got was a five-minute phone call from him, after five weeks of me calling and trying to get ahold of him because I just had to know if these rumors were true and had to hear it straight from the source.

There was nothing. Like he dropped off the planet in my world, but was everywhere else because articles were showing up in all the magazines since he was finishing up a press tour for his new album. And more people than ever were calling me asking for hookups on Foo Fighters concert tickets. Worse yet were all the calls from people who wanted to tell me all the dirt they had on him, like it would comfort me in some way. Whatever. I couldn't escape the thought of him. I purposely didn't watch MTV because his video always seemed to be playing, and I didn't listen to

the radio because his single was climbing the charts. I went grocery shopping a few days after we broke up and heard the elevator-music version
of "Learn to Fly," which gave me an instant stomachache, then saw him
on the cover of *Guitar* magazine staring at me in the check-out line. Like
I wasn't having a hard enough time getting him out of my mind. I didn't
know how to handle it.

I thought, I'm just not that strong. Having a broken heart and a broken leg was more than I could handle in one summer. And I was so scared
that he would change the way I loved people from then on.

Maybe it's my downfall, but I'm one of those girls who will trust you
when I first meet you. I'm easy to take advantage of. When I fall, I fall
hard. But through all of the relationships I've had, I've learned so much
about myself and what kind of person I work best with. I really have no
regrets, although I could definitely pass on some of the heartaches. All I
ask from a guy is that he be honest and truthful. It doesn't seem like too
much to ask, but maybe it is when the guy doesn't know that he's not
being honest and truthful with himself.

There should be a book called "Men Have Cabinets, Women Have
Shelves." That's how I would wrap up my general view on boyfriend relationships. In all of my past experiences, guys are so quick to hide their
feelings and close the door on the situation and easily never speak of it
again. I just wonder, How can they *do* that? I always have my feelings out
there in the open, which makes me vulnerable, I guess, but I have to
address relationship issues so I can see what I have, what's on the shelf,
resolved, before I can move on. But like before, I so easily put my happiness in their hands, and I really have to be careful about that. It took me
several relationships to realize how important it is to be truly happy on
my own and let the next relationship add to my happiness, not depend
on it.

When Dave and I broke up, I didn't leave the house for three days.
I got out my paint set and started painting a picture. I couldn't leave

until it was finished. Since Dave was completely "unavailable" this was the only closure I could figure out on my own. I painted a flower fairy with long red hair and the strongest wings that I could think of—in yellow and gold. The light from her wings reflects a golden glow around her head and the wings hold her up, hovering strongly above a flower garden, which had to have poppies and irises and different kinds of red and pink, and beautiful strong flowers in every form and shape. Her arms cross her chest holding on to her heart. I named the painting "Holding On," which was exactly what I needed to do for a while. Now, when I look at the painting hanging on my wall, I don't see Heartache at all, I see beauty and my innermost strengths in so many layers. That's what it represents to me.

More than ever, I was needing my snowboard girlfriends, especially to get me back riding hard. If I could ride hard. Luckily I have such a great circle of friends who are there for me in the rough times. I'd invested so much time with them on road trips, traveling to competitions, sharing feelings about being the girl riders in the group. For about ten months after I got hurt, I had nightmares leading right up to the moment before I crashed. I kept trying to reverse it and reenacted the jump over and over in my head, thinking, "If only I'd gone faster..." I could have cleared that landing. If I had focused. My girlfriends took me out riding. We rode hard. We rode like we wanted to ride. Flying down fast, stopping only to regroup at the bottom of the mountain, then heading back up for another run and launching down a steep pitch or off into the trees for hidden stashes of powder. Regaining my confidence in riding hard made my bad dreams stop.

When the doctor said my leg was 100 percent healed and I could go back to jumping, my mind wasn't ready yet. The feeling of catching air still scared me. It made me feel breakable and fragile. I was worried about crashing again and misjudging a landing. After my last landing it felt like I went underground and out of the scene. It took so much for me to be where I was, riding on the surface. Jumping made me nervous and I doubted my talents.

Up until this point, I had learned to listen to myself and my gut feeling on every move that I made in my snowboarding career. If I listened carefully, it would lead me back again. So, I thought, start with little jumps that are just there while riding down the mountain—small rollers, natural snowbanks with powder landings. Little airs. I kept doing my physical therapy exercises and riding with my friends, and I felt my lungs again, and my legs were getting stronger. But the hurdle was still in front of me: Could I go back to big air in competition?

There was pressure. My sponsor Sims had stayed with me even though I was unable to compete for a year and missed out on that season's photo shoots. I had to get back on the horse to prove to myself that I could jump again in competition. And I knew I had to do it for my sponsors—to repay them in some way for their support. If not, who knew—when my contract came up for renewal in three months, maybe I'd be the team rider they decided not to keep. At the end of the year, I decided to enter the Sims World Championship 2000 competition up at Whistler Mountain.

It was a nighttime big-air jump—the worst thing to come back into because night events under fluorescent lights meant harder landings, less visibility, extreme cold, and probably an insanely big crowd, especially at Whistler. But my sponsor was the title sponsor of this event and because of the timing, I felt like I had to do it. I talked to some friends who said that I didn't have to do my backside 720—that I had already proved to the world that I could do it and had won a gold for it. Other friends were encouraging me to listen to what I wanted to do. All I knew was I wanted to get back on the horse and prove to myself that I could do it again.

Up at Whistler I was staying with my friend, pro snowboarder Leslee Olson. I remember watching her get ready for competition that day. She was eating a granola bar and listening to music and saying out loud the things she needed to bring up to the mountain: "My helmet, my bib, here's my knee brace..." I had to force every one of those motions and calculate everything she was just doing without much thought. I kept staring at her. That's when I realized, she was in the zone. Leslee was about to jump off a 65-foot big-air jump in front of 20,000 people and it didn't seem to even faze her. It fazed me. I had to get back into it and it wasn't clicking. I had to think everything through. It was calculated. It seemed like I could not find even an ounce of the bravery I once had.

When we got up to the starting gate at the top of the jump, it was already dark outside and lights illuminated the jump for the contest. It was so cold. I felt out of place up there. I was surrounded by all these girls who had competed in fifteen contests previously that season. This was just another big air competition to them. I hadn't been snowboarding in any contest in over a year and felt out of the loop. They were talking about what party they were going to go to after the contest and what guy they thought was cute and I was sitting there thinking, How can they talk so casually? I have to completely visualize and concentrate on this jump or I'm not going to even be able to go down this ramp. Normally I'd be chatting it up with the rest of them, but my mind was so preoccupied with what I was about to do, I could barely engage in any social conversation around me. It took everything I had to just concentrate on my jump.

The first warm-up jumps were scary to think about, and I almost talked myself out of doing them. Somehow, mechanically, I dropped in and rode down the ramp. The speed was good and it felt OK. I popped off the lip and pulled a simple, straight air with a grab. I was feeling better and warming up to the jump. My mind and body started to remember the motions. Things were going along OK, but I didn't want to take anything for granted. I'd only had a few days of jumping something half as big under my belt, because snowparks at ski resorts didn't make jumps this big. There was a band playing at the bottom of the jump (thankfully, not the Foo Fighters, who had been invited by Sims, then mysteriously uninvited, because I would have never made it off the jump if Dave was singing his love songs in the background), so I wasn't listening to my music on my headphones in preparation for the competition jump. I also felt like I needed to hear everything around me. Standing there, up at the top of that jump that night, getting ready to drop in for my first competitive big air since my injury, was one of the hardest moments not only of my career but of my life. If I bombed this, it might cost me my sponsorship and I'd be done with professional snowboarding. I might even crack a legbone, again. Or worse: Never get back on the horse. I was scared to death.

I took in my three deep breaths, feeling cold air burn in my lungs. I dropped in. Speed was good. Just at the lip before I took flight, I could feel it. My bravery was there, my talent was there, and I got my 720 spin around. I could feel myself doing it right, my body remembered. I'd visualized it in my dreams. When I came around, I was a little off and dragged the landing slightly, touching back and didn't stomp it completely. It wasn't my best performance, but I didn't care. I'd done it! For my sponsors, my friends, but mostly myself. I was so incredibly relieved and happy. My score was good enough and I ended up getting second place to Tara Dakides that night.

At the Option Institute, they told me if you let every experience and the people around you add to the happiness that *you* create, then you're doing pretty well. Depending on contest results or sponsors or boyfriends would only set myself up to be let down or disappointed. After that night, I made many decisions—to be more protective of my body, to land on soft snow, to live my life the way that felt right for me.

I still feel my ankle every time I go snowboarding and it gets uncomfortable. That's something new and it's always there. I know what it is— a constant reminder to stay in tune with myself.

stretching to prevent injury

✸ **Stretching is so important in sports.**
It improves flexibility and range of motion, relaxes the
mind, and warms up the body so you're less likely to pull a
muscle. It also aids in recovery and relieves body stiffness.
Remember to always stretch at your own rate and don't
force the stretch past your natural tension. Never bounce or
stretch until it hurts because this can lead to injury. Hold
each stretch at least 10 seconds and breathe in a natural,
relaxing manner. Here are a few stretches to do before you
hit the slopes:

1. Neck stretch— Keeping your head and neck
   facing straight forward, tilt your head to one side in
   slow motion; keeping your shoulders level. Hold
   down for 30 seconds when you feel the natural tension
   of the stretch. Tilt your head back to center and
   then do the same on the other side. Don't jerk your head
   from side to side. Do it three times on each
   side.

2. Calf stretch—Stand two feet away from a wall,
   place both hands against the wall at shoulder height.
   Step back with one foot about two feet, in a lunge
   position, keeping your front leg slightly bent. Keep

your back heel on the ground until you feel the calf stretch. Hold for 30 seconds. Switch sides and repeat three times.

3. Lower back stretch—Lying on your back, bend your left knee at 90 degrees. Extend your arms out to the sides. Place your right hand on your left thigh and pull that bent knee over your right leg, keeping your shoulders flat on the floor. To further the stretch, keep your head on the floor and turn it to face the outstretched arm. Hold for 30 seconds and then switch to your right leg and repeat. Do twice on each side.

4. Hamstring stretch—Lie on your back and place a rope around the ball of one foot. Holding both ends of the rope, lift that leg as high as possible until you feel the stretch. Keep the rope taut and keep your heel aimed toward the ceiling. Keep your shoulders on the floor. Hold the stretch for 30 seconds and then switch legs and repeat. Do twice on each side.

5. Leg stretch—Sit on the floor with both legs stretched out to the sides. With your back straight, not curved, lean toward the floor, extending your arms out in front of you. Keep your neck and head in line with your straight back and hold the stretch for 30 seconds. Do this same motion leaning to each side, stretching your arms over your side and reaching for your foot. Hold 10 seconds and repeat each position twice. ✳

Snowboarding in Alaska.

alaska

Many people wonder why we do it, why we risk so much for what they think is only fame or money. Or risk so much for the ultimate powder run in the backcountry when avalanches could kill you. But all sports have their uncertainties. Snowboarding, like surfing, depends so much on conditions and the weather. Maybe that makes it so much more rewarding in the end—when you finally catch that perfect wave or find that untracked powder run. If it was as easy as going to the local wave pool or indoor ski resort I don't think I would be there every day. Actually, I don't think I would be there at all. It's more than just going through the motions of the sport. Capturing all of those elements it takes to fly down the hill on a snowboard makes you feel so alive. Part of it is the search for that perfect moment when it all comes together. Only the ones who have truly experienced great Alaskan snowboarding will tell you why they do it. It can change your life with a new perspective and simply just be the best time of your life.

In terms of pressure, there aren't thousands of people standing there watching you—it's usually only a filmmaker and a still photographer plus two other snowboarders who fit in the heli. But there's the pressure to perform, Kodak Courage some call it, not only for myself but for my sponsors, because getting your shots in the next season's snowboard video or in the magazines is as important as winning the X Games. Riding in Alaska is not cheap either. A typical day is around $750 for the helicopter time and hiring the guides. But this is my job and how I make my living. I think the real pressure is that you're up against the natural hazards of Mother Nature. Which in an instant can take out your entire group and even the helicopter. Avalanches are real and what everyone fears most. Sometimes it's hard to find the line of how far I should let it go. Risk management to the last degree. But professional athletes' careers are short-lived, and I have to make my mark while I have the chance. There's also the feeling that I can't wimp out. I'm usually the only girl on a heli trip and I want to do every run the guys are doing to show that I can do it, too. This is a different kind of riding—out-of-bounds—and it's important to show that girls don't just rock it in the halfpipe or big air, but that we really do ride like the wind. With experience I learned to choose my days to push it or sometimes just walk away from the run. If I have a bad feeling about it, I'm not doing it. However, it can take a long time to learn to listen to your instincts. Sometimes it's hard to judge that feeling right, and avalanches are unpredictable. My guide once told me, "The more I learn about avalanches, the more I realize I have yet to learn."

If the conditions are right, Alaska is one of those places where you can be the very first to ride down an unknown mountain peak. And if you are the first person to make it down, you get the privilege of naming the mountain, like the ones that were named before such as Hangover Helper and Powder Cakes. I felt ready to face my biggest challenge in Alaska: completing my own first descent. I'm grateful that this moment came after my injury because I was a different, smarter person. My group was up there to shoot with Justin Hostynek for the next snowboarding video and we had photographers with us as well. That day, we were to going to a mountain that was pristine and untouched. We were scoping our lines from the helicopter when Justin's voice came over my headphones in the helicopter, "Tina, do you want this one?" Looking out at this run, it felt right, and I knew that going first while filming with guys, particularly on a first descent, was a great opportunity. I said, "Sure, Justin, I'll do it."

One thing that's clear in Alaska is that even if you do a first descent, the mountain is never your mountain. If you start thinking that way, Mother Nature has a way of smacking you across the face and humbling you to the size of a snowflake. Mother Nature always reminds you who's in charge. And it can be so completely overwhelming. Alaska is bigger than pictures can show—and there are huge risks. The mountain is always moving, cracks forming in the snow, avalanche sounds like low thunder in the distance, and the weather is constantly changing.

When I was getting ready at the top of the mountain, there were so many things going through my head—would my equipment hold up, awareness of avalanches, and concentrating on not making a single mistake. I couldn't. There was no room for a mistake on this one. Plus, I was going first and couldn't blow it and mess up the line for the next guy. I was freezing but took off my gloves to make last-minute adjustments to my bindings to make sure they were tight. I wiped off my goggles and tightened them around my head to make sure I could see clearly, even though from where I was standing, I couldn't see the bottom of the run. It was a bluebird day—what I could see was an entire mountain range that no one had ever stood on before. The wind was cold and sharp, but that wasn't the only thing that caught my breath. I was being told by my guide on the radio strapped to my chest and tucked into my jacket that if the snow started to break off and the slough started to follow me, to keep riding to the right, which would lead me to an exit chute through the exposed rocks, and oh, by the way, don't forget to ollie and jump over the crevasse at the very bottom.

Everything that I'd ever learned in snowboarding I had to use right then and be prepared for any kind of snow condition. It was unpredictable. But I was as prepared as I could be and had everything packed just right in my backpack—my shovel, probe, emergency blanket, extra fleece top, PowerBar, sunscreen, and water. I had to remember all of my previous experience in the backcountry and know how the snow shifts and moves and when to be light on my feet or cross-cut a bowl. I had to visualize my line and remember what I saw from the helicopter when it took me up the mountain and hovered for a few seconds fifteen minutes ago so I could scout my run. Sometimes you can see where you're going, but more often than not the run is blind. I knew I might only be able to see a few turns in front of me and therefore would have to rely on my memory of the run or depend on the guide or photographer across the way to tell me on my radio where I should keep turning.

When I dropped in finally, I didn't want to be totally gripped with fear because I knew from experience that I wouldn't snowboard my best. It's a hard balance to feel the adrenaline rush while being gripped and just wanting to get down the mountain. I knew the camera was on and I was being filmed as I made my first turns of the run. Knowing the faster I went, the better it would look on film, I picked up my speed and really went for it. The feeling of the untracked powder under my board as I was flying down the run was amazing. The glittering snowflakes flew in plumes off the side of my board as I made my turns. I could see every detail of the snow because it was a crystal clear bluebird day. Once in a while I would look out on the horizon and glimpse through my goggles the amazing view I saw from the top and would think about these ancient glaciers I was riding, then remember to be light, very light, and keep breathing. I knew the minute I let my guard down or thought everything was going OK, something enormous could happen. I was so small riding down this huge mountain and had to keep turning, remembering to look back every couple of seconds to see if any snow was moving with me.

Almost at the bottom, I felt this incredible rush of having done a first descent. This was definitely one of the best powder runs of my entire life. When I got to the bottom, I sighed with relief that I'd made it down, and what an accomplishment! I named the mountain "T-top." I looked back up at my turns and the run I just came down and could barely believe it. A smile crossed my face. I felt emotional, but the extraordinary feeling of relief that I had done it safely overpowered my emotions. I couldn't tell if I was going to cry or laugh, and I just kept smiling.

We rode longer in the day because of the midnight sun, but seven unbelievable powder runs in a full day, from 8 A.M. to 8 P.M., plus the movement from flying in the helicopter, is enough to make you dizzy. I was totally exhausted and my mind was completely tapped. But there was nothing better than that feeling.

That time things were good and some people may think I was lucky. Since then, there have been near tragedies. One season was particularly bad. There had been a few people who had died up there and the snow conditions spooked everyone. I was there with our guides from Out of Bounds Adventures and filming with Justin, and we'd picked this line, scoped it out from the heli, along with the other riders in my group, Axel Pauporte and Mark Frank. We had decided the order of the run would be Justin first so he could go set up for the shoot, then Mark, Axel, and me. The helicopter dropped us off and we crouched down with our gear and waited for it to lift off. Right after the heli started to rise, our radios exploded with the voice of the helicopter pilot, "It's gone, it's gone! The whole thing is gone!" About seven feet away from where we were standing there was a fracture line going across the entire mountain where we had just scoped our lines. We couldn't see any farther than this fracture line. Axel took one step forward to try to see what had happened and backed up quickly. He said the whole thing had slid—the entire mountainside had avalanched.

The pressure from the heli blades just landing had released this fracture, called a climax fracture, which means it cracked off all the snow all the way down to the dirt, rock, and ice, sending the entire side of the mountain sliding all the way across the entire bowl. The avalanche had gone 3,500 feet down to the glacier below.

We stayed put and didn't move; there was no other way down the mountain. There was no snow left to even ride. We had to wait for the helicopter to come back and pick us up. We were all very quiet and just waited. When the heli arrived, we loaded in and when it swung around the front of the mountain, we could see where our lines had been and there was nothing left. I gasped. It was a weird freaky feeling because if any of us had dropped into that bowl, it would have released and we would not have survived.

That was the first time that I could really feel in my gut the risk involved with riding in Alaska. We knew the risks, but seeing it right there just minutes before we were to ride down brought it all back into the forefront of my mind. It made me ask myself how much I was willing to risk. Am I willing to die for it? What the hell am I doing up here anyway? I kept going back and forth and thought about it constantly.

From then on, riding in Alaska was different for me. Every morning before I would leave my hotel room to head to the heli-pad, I would make sure it was organized and neat, just in case I didn't come back. I don't know why, but I didn't want it to be too much work for the maid if it was messy. The fear of dying made it so hard to grab my snowboard and backpack and walk out the door for another day of heli snowboarding. It was hard to snap back into the right mind-set and feel confident enough in my riding that I could even do this. Sometimes I would still be talking myself into it at the top of the first run. I knew I had to be brave. Each night I would call home because my mom and dad were always waiting for my call.

Last spring in Alaska, I couldn't have predicted what would happen. I thought at this point I was at the "less-risk" phase of my life, but of course, every time I think that, there's another challenge. I'd just come back from recovering from an eye-socket fracture. I had been filming for a feature film called *Keep Your Eyes Open* ironically. I was doing a big-air jump—everyone wanted to film the 720. The snow was too soft and slow on the takeoff and when I landed, I crashed hard and bounced onto my face. I wasn't able to drive for two weeks because I was seeing double. But when Justin called to film in Alaska, I pulled it together. My mother gave me essential oils that I applied daily and the swelling in my face had gone down and the black and blue was almost gone. Still, things were a little blurry, especially when I would get tired.

❋ *Threading my way through the crevasse field in Juneau, Alaska.*

I flew into Alaska straight from launching our first Boarding for Breast Cancer event in Japan, complete with a bruised eye. It was a twelve-hour flight and I got off the plane in Haines, Alaska, at 11 A.M., and found myself in the Out of Bounds Adventures helicopter going up the mountain at two that afternoon. My film crew was Justin, along with Axel and Yannick, who were top big-mountain riders from France. Riding that day was probably not the smartest thing to do, but I wanted some of those runs so badly and I had called in several times from Japan about the weather in Haines and heard it was clearing up and they were flying. So there I was. At the top of the run, tired and a little blurry, but Justin was going to film me going down this finger chute that was narrow but a great run that I knew I could do. It was super steep and the snow conditions changed my third turn into the run and it just bucked me unexpectedly and I started to tumble. I flipped head over heels once, then twice, trying to stop my momentum the whole time. The run was too steep and now I was cartwheeling head over heels down the entire mountain. I remember at this point covering my head with my hands when I fell. I couldn't see anything. It was the worst fall I've ever taken. At the bottom, I finally came to a stop. I thought, Holy shit, I'm so glad that's over with. I looked back up at the run and realized that I had just missed hitting rocks by a couple of feet and was lucky that I didn't tumble over any cliffs. I was jet-lagged but was now wide awake. I'd never taken a fall like that before and it hit me that I could have just died. It spooked me and I knew I couldn't ride in this frame of mind, so I flew home the next day.

My instincts have also kicked in at just the right moment and saved my life. Again, I was filming with Justin and came down the first run of the day, and on my third turn, I could feel the snow shift and saw this huge crack shoot out in either direction right under my board. I knew it was an avalanche. I had to get out of there and quickly rode to the right of the slope, which was where we had scoped our safe zone and the only exit if trouble started. From my safe zone, I watched as the slab of snow funneled down the chute I had been riding. If I hadn't exited when I did, I would have had no other choice but to try and outrun the slide. It was a blind run and I couldn't see that it had triggered into an entire avalanche. In my panic to contact my guide, I somehow turned off my radio and thought my batteries had died. The only person in voice range from where I was stuck was Yannick, who was at the bottom of the run and off to the right. Unfortunately, he speaks French and only a little English. He yelled up at me, "Come down, come down, Tina!" and motioned with his hands where I should ride, so I'd take some turns and stop and try to follow his hands. As soon as I could see the safe line down the rest of the mountain, I rode as fast as I could out of there. We continued on with our day of filming, and I tried not to let it affect my mind-set, but it was there.

I didn't see the footage that Justin had shot of the avalanche until three months later. In the film you can see this whole mountain moving with snow, pluming over cliffs as it travels down the chute. And there I am, this little speck in the frame waiting over to the right above some rocks, watching it all happen. It was scary to watch and it brought chills and made me nervous all over again. I had no idea it was that big of a slide. Alaska can make you feel so small and then in the next instant, after an incredible run, you can feel bigger than life.

Managing that calculated risk takes a weird balance. We've always had excellent guides up there and have been willing to risk a little bit. I say now, it's worth part of the risk. I was definitely in situations where if it had avalanched out I would have been stuck with no safe zone to go to, no exit chute, rocks exposed. When I think of some of the risky runs I've had in Alaska, I sometimes wonder, "What was I thinking?" But when you ride your best, leaving Alaska gives you that sense of having survived accompanied by a sense of accomplishment. It's such a weird zone to be in when you have to be at your peak performance level. You need to be as confident as possible but humble, because of where you are and what you're about to do. I'm not an adrenaline junkie and not in it for the rush. I'm not the crazy adrenaline type of athlete. I do it more for the soulful feeling of going down the mountain and having done something thought impossible. That's what gets me to keep going back.

a day of helicopter snowboarding

✹ Just being around a helicopter is dangerous. Any heli-ski service will make you go through an orientation to learn the rules and proper etiquette of being around a helicopter. This is so important because one person can make a mistake and it can be a disaster for the whole group. A flyaway hat can get caught in the rotor blades and cause a helicopter to crash. A helicopter is a delicate piece of machinery.

The sound of a heli starting up gives me a rush of excitement because it means I'm going for some powder runs. Even the smell of the fuel can get my adrenaline flowing. I love sitting in the front of the helicopter with the guide and the pilot. I usually luck out with that seating position because I'm usually the lightest weight in the group and need to be toward the front of the ship. In Alaska, you just point to a mountain and the pilot will take you there. The pilot will hover in front of the run so each rider can scope out a line and get a good look at it before

we head to the top to get dropped off. We even take
Polaroid pictures to help remember the runs when we get
to the top. Often the runs are completely blind, meaning all
you can see from the top is the mountain just rolling away
into nothing. You can't see your whole run to the bottom.
Those are the scariest runs and you really have to trust
your judgment and remember your point of reference, like
a rock or cornice. Sometimes you can have the filmer (who
is usually set up
across the valley)
guide you into
the correct chute
by radio. The
backcountry is
so unpredictable,
so we always
have a guide with
us to help us
decide the safest
lines and what to

*Working on my graphics in
my hotel room in Alaska.*

expect from the snow conditions.
Because of avalanche dangers we
always pick the islands of safety before we drop in to a
run. These are areas that are safe from avalanches, like a
group of trees or below a rocky area of the mountain. If
you start an avalanche on the run, you ride to the nearest
island of safety to get out of the way. Heli-snowboarding is
not cheap—a typical heli day is around $750. But if you
can save up and get your friends together to do it, it can
be the most memorable riding of your life. ✱

what to pack in your backpack for a day in the backcountry

1. Water in a plastic bottle—it's so important to stay hydrated.

2. A lunch and a snack—my favorites are Lunchables and a peanut butter Tiger bar.

3. Sunscreen is a must, even on stormy days. It's always good to have it in your pack in case the weather changes.

4. Chapstick with a sunscreen in it.

5. A compass—even on what looks like a sunny day. If the weather comes in, it is easy to lose your way.

6. A shovel to help rescue victims of an avalanche and also to build huge kickers in the backcountry.

7. A backcountry blanket. If you ever have to stay in the woods overnight this can save your life.

8. An extra layer of clothing in case the weather changes or you get your first layer wet.

9. Extra goggles, if you have them. I've lost many pairs of goggles from crashing so hard that you just can't find them in the snow. Also, it's great to have a fresh pair to throw on while waiting for the wet ones to dry out.

10. A camera. This is optional, but it's always in my backpack. I can never pass up a great group shot at the top of a mountain.

11. A probe to check for rocks on the landings and to help find someone buried in an avalanche.

12. If you are carrying a cell phone, turn it off until you are in a safe zone or need to make an emergency call. Cell phone signals can sometimes interfere with avalanche transceivers.

Make sure to find a backpack that has a hip strap. This helps take the weight off your shoulders and keeps the pack from swinging around when you ride. ✳

avalanche safety tips

1. Always wear an avalanche beacon when snowboarding in the backcountry, test it, and know how to use it before heading up to the mountain.

2. Check the avalanche report by calling the local hotline before making the decision to head into the backcountry.

3. Never hike right up the middle of an open bowl or snow, or underneath cornice ridges. And never walk out on a cornice to look below.

Waiting for the heli to pick us up, Alaska.

4. Determine your main islands of "safety" before you drop in. These are usually clusters of trees or rocky areas of the mountain that have less potential of sliding.

5. When snowboading with a group, ride one at a time and regroup at an island of safety.

6. Ski-cut a face to test the stability of the snow.

7. Avalanche dangers are usually high after a large snowstorm. And check the wind patterns—they can add to overloading of snow on a slope and make it unsafe.

8. When the weather warms up, it adds to the potential of slides.

9. Never hike or stop on a run underneath another group of riders.

10. Always listen to your surroundings and be alert. ✳

PLAYBOY

Dear Tina,

Hope this letter finds you doing well and hitting the slopes in Utah! Enclosed please find a few issues that might help you to familiarize yourself with the type of content and photography we produce. Although none of the features will look exactly like the *Women of Extreme Sports* , they should give you a general idea and feeling.

As you can tell the photography is always of the highest standards and quality. For years it is always been our goal to photograph the women we feature issue after issue in the most complimentary style and fashion.

For the last 45 year Playboy has photographed and featured some of the biggest names in the world. Names like; Katarina Witt, Cindy Crawford, Pamela Anderson, Sharon Stone, Farrah Fawcett, Stephanie Seymoure, Elle Macpherson, Naomi Campbell and Marilyn Monroe just to name a few.

Please call me after you've had an opportunity to look the issues over.

Sincerely,

Kevin Kuster

Kevin Kuster
Associate Photo Editor
Playboy Magazine

mainstream

In the eighteen years that I'd been snowboarding, the sport had grown up and was turning into a worldwide business. No one ever imagined that it would catch on and grow this fast. I had no idea that I would still be snowboarding professionally this long. Because mainstream America was getting more involved in snowboarding, our sponsors had investors outside of the snowboarding industry and some snowboard manufacturers had even gone public.

Around the time of the first few X Games, snowboard companies had much bigger budgets than they were used to and we were rollin' as their sponsored athletes and began to take it for granted that we had made it as snowboarders. We thought this would last forever. One of our team photo shoots for Sims cost $60,000, because we were ordering room service and wine and we were staying at a five-star resort. I went from traveling on road trips in motor homes stocked with Price Club food to staying at five-star hotels, even flying in a Beech jet.

One night, Sims was having an opening party for their new office in Los Angeles and invited me down. Since I was completely traveled out at the time from several competitions and photo shoots, I called to tell them that I just couldn't get on another flight. John Textor, Sims's former owner, had a Beech jet that he graciously flew the team around in every once in a while. He called and said, "You've got to come down here—you're a big part of this team. I'll send the jet up there to get you." At the private airport in Sacramento I was sitting there among a crowd of all these rich guys in suits who were also waiting for their jets to come pick them up. I was in my Hurley hooded sweatshirt and my backpack. I walked up to the check-in counter, and they asked, "Which plane is yours?" I guess they were asking for the number of the jet or something, but I didn't understand. I said, "It's a jet with blue and gold stripes on the sides." The man at the counter laughed and replied, "That's not going to help us much, honey." I admit I was a little out of my element. but maybe they just weren't ready for us snowboarders yet.

The pilots were super nice and let me sit up front in the cockpit. I actually got to fly the jet for about fifteen minutes. I put the headphones on and did a 1,200-foot descent into L.A. Of course I didn't land the plane, but it was pretty fun and I had a great story to tell when I got to the party.

It was the heyday of snowboarding, the late '90s, and snowboarding industry trade shows had booths with DJs and models passing out stickers and it wasn't unusual to see celebrities or musicians in the halls checking things out. Snowboard manufacturers would throw extravagant parties and hire bands like the Fugees and the Strokes. It was important for us to be at all of these trade shows because we were representing the image that was part of our obligation to our sponsors now. Our image was what was being used to sell products. It was also a blast to be there

❄ *Skydiving for a TV show.*
"Look, Michael, I did it!"

because it was one of the few times a year that we got to see all of the snowboarders and our friends in the industry without being at a competition, which meant we didn't have to get up early, so we would party the night away. Someone was always the victim of the Permanent Marker Treatment. This might be something only snowboarders do, but whoever passed out first was doomed to get drawn on by their friends with a black Sharpie. It was always funny to see someone the next day at the trade show with "Shred head" written across their forehead.

At first, the core group of professional snowboarders and people in the industry didn't agree with the new path snowboarding was taking. Like them, I was worried that people would forget that snowboarding had its own history, soul, and culture. Some businesspeople were now obviously in it for the cool image and the money. New snowboard brands were popping up by companies that didn't have any clue what our culture was all about. It seemed like everyone wanted a piece of it. People who didn't even know how to ride were starting snowboard companies. Even ski companies started making snowboards. There were "extreme" pizza joints popping up, and fashion spreads in *Vogue* with models carrying boards, and ridiculous window treatments at the Gap that misrepresented our culture with signs that read "Shred sale." They might as well have had the models wear Day-Glo, or a one-piece ski suit.

I wondered if mainstream America even knew that at one time it was our parents who helped run those first contests, or if they remembered snowboarders like Terry Kidwell and Damian Sanders who helped push the path of snowboarding toward freestyle. These were my heroes, but who were theirs? And did they have any or even care?

Opportunities for male and female snowboarders were moving in many different directions, everyone was turning pro, and we were all making money. As pros, we had top-of-the-line snowmobiles, new cars, and tons of snowboarding gear. High-end equipment, apparel, and accessories were now so available to us that when kids at snowboard contests would

If it snowed, everyone showed up at my house in Utah.

approach us, we would generously give our gear away knowing that we could get more. So we couldn't complain too much. I now owned my own house in Utah that was big enough to fit all of my snowboarding friends. When it snowed, people would just show up. People knew where my Hide-A-Key was and I welcomed friends anytime.

I also started receiving more fan letters. One was from a girl from southern California who had written a letter and sent it to Airwalk for me. She'd seen me ride in a contest on TV and wanted to share her snowboarding experiences with me and complimented my riding. It was the coolest feeling getting that letter and I wrote her back. We stayed in touch for a few years. Over the years I've made lots of new pen pals with kids who have written me letters. I was honored that they'd want to write and share their stories. It was nice to see so many young people loving snowboarding the way I did.

I wanted to take every opportunity that came my way as a new experience because I loved snowboarding so much, but learned the hard way to be cautious about the side effects that the mainstream views would have on my career. I once agreed to be on an MTV Sports event called the "Icey Cool Plunge." I was supposed to skim on my snowboard across a 50-foot pond of water that was surrounded by crowds of people. I had never skimmed across water before on my snowboard and ended up going way too fast because I was worried that I might sink if I went too slow like the guy who went before me, and skidded out on the water and went crashing into the crowd, knocking over at least fifteen people. It felt like I had broken both of my legs at the time. I thought, I cannot believe this is what would take me out of snowboarding. I ended up being OK with only bruised shins and a bruised ego from hitting people. It was all caught on camera and showed on TV. It was a mainstream opportunity I should have passed up.

From then on I realized that if I was to be the new spokesperson for "Extreme Pizza" or something cheesy, it could have damaged my reputation because it was so obviously uncool. Although, when I was asked to be animated in four different video games with Infogrammes and Konami out of Japan, this was one of those cool new opportunities. I wasn't much of a video game player, but the whole process of helping to create myself as a video game character was unique. The video game producers would watch videotapes of me snowboarding, then had me critique all of the steps involved in making tricks in a game. I even did voice-overs for the sound effects. So when my character crashes in the game, it's really my voice saying "Ouch" or "Watch out!" However, shooting one of the commercials for the video game promotion was an odd experience because it involved going to a vacant cheese factory in New Jersey and pretending

Shooting the video game commercial with Peter Line and Todd Richards at a vacant cheese factory somewhere in New Jersey.

to snowboard on Astro Turf that was rotating on a big conveyor belt. I was with pro snowboarders Todd Richards and Peter Line and we were laughing the whole time because this couldn't have been further from what snowboarding was really about. But since it supported our new games, we wanted to be a part of it. Concessions of a professional athlete.

Other riders were branching out and getting mainstream sponsors like Nike, Ralph Lauren, Subaru, and Mountain Dew. I never got any big-time offers for sponsorship with any mainstream company, but my friends and I were hired to snowboard in mainstream commercials. I turned down the Tampax snowboarding commercial, but did "Do the Dew"

Wearing a wig for the Mountain Dew commercial.

on my snowboard for a one-time gig for a Mountain Dew commercial filmed in Jackson Hole, Wyoming. I had never had my hair and makeup done before heading out to go ride, but this was a Hollywood shoot, complete with people assigned just to get you a cup of coffee. I barely snowboarded and waited around all day for the shoot.

When *Playboy* magazine called (they'd seen the Dew) and asked me to pose for their "Extreme" issue, my first reaction was "Hell, no!" Then my curiosity led me to call them back. I asked my parents how they would feel about it, explaining to them that it would be the highest quality photography and I would be represented as an athlete with an action snowboarding shot, and an interview alongside of my poseur shot, and maybe I could talk about Boarding for Breast Cancer. They both said it should be my decision. But after I hung up, my dad called back about twenty seconds later to confirm that I would be in my bathing suit. Two weeks later I received five issues of *Playboy* in the mail to "review." The first picture I opened up to was a female jockey with her pants around her ankles getting weighed in on a scale. I quickly realized that wearing a bathing suit was probably not an option and there was no way I belonged in *Playboy*.

Snowboarding was gaining exposure fast on other levels, too. New events were popping up like the MTV Sports and Music Festival and Half-pipe Contest with a $100,000 first-place prize. Top snowboarders were getting enticed to participate because of the exposure and prize money. We were asked to be a part of things like MTV road trips, or present at

First place at the MTV Snowed In big-air contest, Snow Summit, California, 1999.

award ceremonies like the ESPN Sports and Music Awards. When I presented the Snowboarder of the Year award in 2001 with Daryl Hannah and Paul Walker, I didn't know what to expect. ESPN sent a limo to pick me and my friends up and take us to the venue. When they dropped us off at the red carpet, there were TV cameras everywhere and paparazzi taking photos. It's pretty cool when the red carpet is filled with skateboarders, snowboarders, and surfers. Quite a colorful bunch of people. I wondered what the world thought of us now.

With Daryl Hannah and Astrid at ESPN's Action Sports and Music Awards show.

After the show, I met the musicians in Metallica, who were there to accept an award for being Snowboarders' Favorite Band. They were part of my culture and I often listened to their music before a contest to get psyched up. I don't think they knew that snowboarders listened to them so much and they were surprised that we were such fans. It was by far one of the best perks for being a celebrity snowboarder.

But I couldn't help but wonder if all of this attention meant we were really respected or if now we were considered just the flavor of the month, the new rockstars of sports. It did have a ripple effect, however. Snowboarding, along with other action sports like surfing and skateboarding, was becoming the future for youth culture. It's changed traditional sports.

❄ *Hanging out*
with James Hetfield
of Metallica at the
ESPN awards show.

More kids today skateboard than play baseball. I'm now a part of a bigger group of athletes other than just snowboarders. My sponsors branched out, and now my teammates include surfers, skateboarders, and motocross riders. We're friends and can all relate to the pressures of competing, traveling, and sponsorships. We all share stories like one big family and often influence each other with our own experiences in our specific sports. Freestyle motocross riders are pulling backflips like snowboarders, and snowboarders often name new tricks after skateboarding moves. Surfers are now grabbing their boards in tricks that are influenced by snowboarders—who grab their boards doing moves similar to skateboarders.'

Like the dotcom bust or any new industry that grows too fast, we could also crash. Just a few years after the peak of our heyday, things changed. In 2000 and 2001 Japan got flooded with too much product—now gear was not moving and was just sitting on the shelves in snowboard shops. This had a big effect on us because a third of our business was in Japan. Outside investors who didn't have their hearts in snowboarding would easily pull the plug and shut down companies after one bad selling season. I had friends who hopped onboard as team riders with brand-new companies that claimed to have deep pockets, only to get cut along with their entire team. I was lucky that I always made the cuts on the team because my sponsors supported women's product, which isn't necessarily the case with other sports. My sponsors saw the importance of this. It also helped that I had a positive attitude. I'd seen so many up-and-coming kids complaining about doing things for their sponsors like expense reports or bitching about how much other snowboarders were making compared with them. Sponsors get turned off by that quickly. So they'd get the boot. Attitude is everything.

Our sport is also very dependent on the weather. A bad snow season could result in product not moving and immediately impact teams taking pay cuts and downsizing. Even though one year I only sold 1,500 snowboards because it was a bad snow season and the shops had leftover product from the year before, I had momentum from being in the sport so long and my sponsors saw the value in the exposure I was getting as a female athlete for their brand. It's weird when the business side of your career depends not only on the economy, but so heavily on the weather and those snowflakes that miraculously fall out of the sky. When it's a snowy day, goggle sales go up. If it snows early in the season, boards start selling, and if there's no snow over the Christmas holiday, ski resorts lose money. Lots of money. In my world, snowflakes make the world go 'round. That's just the wave of snowboarding.

Good or bad, the image of snowboarding was making an impact on other sports that I didn't expect. Gaylene Nagel from Sims, who now worked at EA Sports, a video game publisher, called me one day to participate in a promotional gig in Los Angeles for the snowboarding video game SSX. They said that Tiger Woods would be there and EA wanted to know if I would come down and participate. I thought, Of course I would, and maybe, I thought to myself, I could even get to meet Tiger. So I flew into L.A. and spent the night at the Ritz Carlton (EA doesn't mess around). In the morning the publicist from EA came and picked me up and we went for breakfast before the promotion. Over breakfast I said to her, "I heard that Tiger Woods is going to be at the trade show. Do you think I can get a picture with him? Because I brought my camera." She looked at me and said, "Honey, has anyone told you what you're doing today?" I told her I thought it was going to be like a trade show and all the athletes would be there, signing autographs and playing the EA video games. She said, "No, you're in a photo shoot with Tiger Woods for the front page of *USA Today*. There is no trade show—the photo shoot is set up in one of the suites upstairs."

We walked into this room and there was Tiger Woods with all his peeps. I was star-struck and shyly introduced myself. He looked me right in the eye, shook my hand, and said, "So, you're the pro." It was one of those stares that make you look away at first. He had such confidence that it filled the room. They sat us chair-to-chair, knee-to-knee, and we each had a video game controller in our hands. We were promoting the snowboarding video game because the Tiger Woods video game was off-season or something, but they still wanted him present. In the background they had the snowboarding game playing on the big-screen TV and the idea was that he and I were supposed to look at each other competitively like we were playing the game.

We were talking to each other while the photographer was getting ready and he asked me a little bit about snowboarding, mentioning that he might try it someday. I told him I'd only been golfing three times before and wasn't much of a fan of golf, but thought he was excellent. We talked about sponsors and I tried to get him to trade watches with me. I figured his watch was given to him by one of his sponsors and it was much nicer than mine, which I told him I'd give him. I figured he could probably get another one, but he didn't go for it.

It was already a pretty surprising day, but then the TV show *Access Hollywood* showed up and they wanted us to play the video game. It was a timed racing snowboarding game and being the freestyler that I am, I was doing tricks while I was racing and joking around like, "Hey, did you

see that backflip I just did?" And Tiger would say, "So, what place are you in?" I was always in second. He was not about to let me win even at my own game.

I think he would be good at anything he tried. He's one of those people who are gifted with talent, which made me think of where talent comes from. Anyone can work out and become strong and get into sports and learn. You can practice and practice and it makes you near perfect. You can learn these movements of your sport and teach your body these motions. So, it's hard to know where the true talent part comes in. Tiger Woods is the greatest golfer ever. He's been preparing and programming his body and mind his whole life to perform, and the result is that he's labeled one of the most talented athletes in the world. I cannot imagine what that would be like. I wondered if in the future there would ever be a snowboarder with that sort of dedication their entire life.

We didn't get the front page of *USA Today*, because Matt Damon scooped it from us for some movie promo. But we ended up with a nice full-page article, and I did end up getting my snapshot photo with him in the end.

happy monkeys

❋ I was honored to be able to work
with artist and designer Paul Frank on snowboard graphics
and an animated short film. Paul Frank's artistic talent is
a part of who he is. He has an amazing imagination and
each of his cartoon caricatures that he creates has a
personality and really seems to come to life. His designs
for clothing, accessories, furniture, and art creations are
his own style—he'd be making them whether other people
were into them or not. That's what I think is a cool thing
about Paul Frank.

❋ *My cartoon
character.*

I was asked to be a part of an animated cartoon
he created called *Julius and Friends*. They wrote up a
little script and asked me to do a voice-over for the

snowboard character with red hair and freckles (me) who went on a snowboarding adventure with Julius the Monkey and his friends. The three-minute short film involved all the animals, including a monkey, raccoon, and giraffe piling onto my snowboard and flying down the hill on one wild ride that leads us into an unexpected encounter with the Shaka Bra Yeti, Paul Frank's version of the abominable snowman. The cartoon premiered at the Sundance Film Festival in 2001, which was an amazing thing to be a part of. Lisa Hudson and I went out to Park City, Utah, to see the screening of the cartoon. It was so cool to see it premiering at such a prestigious film festival. The creation was a breath of fresh air amidst all the dark and artsy cartoons out there today. It received Honorable Mention at the festival. From that cartoon came the idea to create snowboard graphics with Paul Frank using his *Julius and Friends* characters and the little girl with the red hair and freckles. ✳

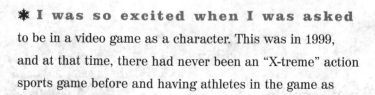

creating a video game character

✳ **I was so excited when I was asked** to be in a video game as a character. This was in 1999, and at that time, there had never been an "X-treme" action sports game before and having athletes in the game as characters was a new idea. Tony Hawk's game wasn't even out yet. I remember Lisa Hudson asked me to come into her office so she could show me to her boss. She said, "This

❋ *My video game character.*

is Tina, she's a professional athlete, and I think we should put her in a snowboarding game." Sounds like the normal thing to do, but back then it needed backup. So we brought in professional snowboarder Peter Line. Peter, being the gamer that he is, completely related to the video game developers and talked about ideas that you could do for different levels of riding and different locations. He went on and on . . .

They went for it. The first snowboarding video game was to be made and called "Pro Boarder." I imagined them hooking us up with sensors and wires and jumping on trampolines inside a warehouse or somewhere, trying to do tricks. That was not possible because it wouldn't look right.

Lucky for the athletes, some of the video game designers actually snowboarded and knew what was up. They watched videotapes and had us critique all of the steps involved with making tricks in a game. We even did voice-overs for the sound effects. So it's really my voice saying "Ouch" or "Watch out!"

We did our first promotion of the game out at the Winter X Games in Vermont in 1999. It was the weirdest experience watching kids play my character   when they would crash, they'd look back and say "Sorry, Tina." I just replied, "It's OK. It doesn't hurt." ✳

*Rooting for Shannon
at the 2002 Winter
Olympics in Park
City, Utah.*

C H A P T E R   1 6

olympics

If it weren't for the X Games getting us publicity, telecasting to 110 million people worldwide, I don't know if the Olympics would ever have considered snowboarding. We were by far the most outcast sport in the world and definitely didn't fit into the rigid, old-school format of the Olympic Games. Snowboarders had green hair, multiple piercings, and tattoos. We used words like rip, slash, ally-oop, and indy grabs. The thing was that many countries had snowboarding competitions, which is one of the prerequisites for a sport to become an Olympic event. There was an established World Cup snowboarding tour and it could not be denied that it was a full-fledged business. In the first ten years it had grown 237 percent and up to $82 million in board sales.

The X Games also let the mainstream public see snowboarding. Snowboarding was now popular at ski resorts and it was not out of the ordinary to see all types of people out on the hill trying it. The ratio of skiers to snowboarders was almost equal. I thought it was cool to see whole families out snowboarding and kids as young as five learning how to snowboard before they even knew how to ski. Looking around at all the snowboarders at the ski resorts, I couldn't believe that I used to have to explain what a snowboard was. It gave our sport a huge boost and provided grounds for more commitment from sponsors. It helped establish snowboarding as a legitimate sport and its professionals as legitimate athletes, whether the Olympics thought this or not. When the Olympics finally allowed snowboarding, it was the final seal of approval—snowboarding was something everyone would have to accept. We were mainstream and here to stay.

The first time snowboarding was an event in the Olympics was for the Nagano, Japan, Olympic Games in 1998. I tried out for the halfpipe team, but I was already two years out of competing consistently in the halfpipe. There were only two events available in the 1998 Olympics for snowboarders, which were giant slalom and halfpipe. I was doing well in the slopestyle and had just won the big air in the X Games, but those disciplines weren't considered for an Olympic event. Timing is everything. I wish snowboarding would have been considered for the Olympics back when I was competing well in the halfpipe on the World Cup tour. I didn't make the Olympic team but I wasn't too bummed because I was already moving on to big air. If big air was an Olympic event then, I may have been a medal contender.

Anyway, some of my friends, like professional snowboarder Terje Haakonsen, refused to participate in the Olympics for many reasons, mainly because the Olympics had their own rules and regulations for the sport that were not what we had created in snowboarding. The first reaction to snowboarding in the Olympics was that it would take the soul out of the sport. The thought of coaches, trainers, and uniforms wasn't what snowboarding was all about. But soon I realized that this could be an opportunity to have our sport recognized as an Olympic event, which fundamentally was considered the pinnacle of sports. This could finally give us the respect we so eagerly longed for in our sport and as athletes. My girlfriend Shannon made the team and won the bronze medal in Nagano and reported that the Olympics was an incredible experience because it brought worldwide athletes from all sorts of disciplines together. It was a different way to communicate other than through governments. Athletes from around the world, representing their countries, could share for two weeks the feeling of sport and being the best athletes they could be. Unfortunately, I think the only thing the world noticed about our sport in the Nagano Games was Ross Rebagliati from Canada, who had his gold medal taken away for a positive drug test. This was blown way out of proportion and the media focused on this incident, again giving snowboarding a bad reputation. It was like, See, those punk kids really didn't fit in. Although an international arbitration board later voted to return the gold medal to Ross, the message seemed to be that, even with an established event like the Olympics, we were still on our own.

I think snowboarding was different from other sports in the Olympics because of the individual people who were a part of it. I could really tell the difference from my experience of almost becoming an Olympic trainee for gymnastics. In gymnastics, the pressure already existed and it was an established sport in many countries. You knew what the steps were and the competitive pressures it took to overcome to make it to the top. Snowboarding was new and unpredictable. The pressure wasn't established yet. In snowboarding, a new girl could easily work her way onto the scene and get into competitive series like the Vans Triple Crown of Snowboarding, and make it all the way to the Olympics on her own. Now there's more pressure to get to the top. Kids look up to Shannon Dunn and her accomplishments in Nagano for what she's done in the halfpipe. They don't even know all of the other things she's done for the sport. These kids can go train in snowboard school with coaches and trainers and take the typical traditional route to the Olympics. From now on, competitive snowboarding will be a different experience with different goals.

When the Olympics were coming to the United States in 2002, I knew I had to go watch just to witness the full circle our sport had made. I went to watch the women's halfpipe with my soon-to-be boyfriend Cory. This was our first date, and we spent the whole morning making "Go for the Gold Shannon" signs. This was the first time I felt like a fan going to support my snowboarding girls. We had to park so far away and walk with the crowds of people through security checkpoints. I remember thinking there was no way all of these people could possibly be here for the snow-

Cory and I entering the scaffolding seating at the 2002 Olympics in Park City, Utah.

boarding halfpipe event. When we entered the massive scaffolding seating arena, it hit me: All of these people holding American flags, regardless of whether they knew a single thing about snowboarding or not, were here to support our girls. It was an amazing feeling. I just stared at the halfpipe. It was perfectly shaped. I told Cory the story of my first halfpipe contest at Donner Ski Ranch and I couldn't believe that this was where it had led to, sitting there with 20,000 other people, cheering on our friends who were competing for the gold medal. I was completely absorbed in it. I got chills when they would call out the competitors' names and I screamed the whole time holding up my signs. This was history in the making.

Kelly Clark won the gold in the halfpipe, our first U.S. gold of the Games. In the men's halfpipe the following day, the U.S. guys—Ross Powers, Danny Kass, and J.J. Thomas—would sweep all the top podium spots for the first time in forty-seven years for the USA.

I always feel grateful that I was able to see snowboarding from the beginning and watch it take shape and come full circle at the Olympics. The negative attitude toward snowboarding from Nagano had been erased. Now the world knew what snowboarding was all about. We were truly legitimate athletes.

The photo chosen for the book Gameface.

girls rock

Nadia Comaneci was my only sports hero growing up. One of the few times my parents brought the TV out of the closet was so we could see her performances at the Montreal Olympics and watch a historic moment for women in sports.

Twenty-two years later, in 1998, I was invited to the launch party for *Women's Sports & Fitness* magazine in New York, where they were celebrating women in sports. I didn't know Nadia was going to be there, but there she was, in the same room I was in. I introduced myself and completely fumbled my words and kept saying the same thing over and over, "You're my hero ... I've always admired you ... you're my hero ..."

Nadia was so nice and we talked for a few minutes. She gave me advice on the importance of sticking with what you love without letting the pressure get to you, and wished me luck with my snowboarding. At the end of the party the magazine introduced all of the athletes and brought them onto the stage. I was so proud to be standing on the same stage with volleyball player Gabriella Reece, surfer Lisa Anderson, professional basketball players, tennis players...and Nadia. I will never forget that moment.

I'd been a professional snowboarder for seventeen years (whether I was considered an athlete or not) and still could not believe the doors that snowboarding continued to open for me. I'd met Nadia, played video games with Tiger, heli-boarded in Alaska, won a gold medal at the X Games. But what I was most proud of was that my little snowboarding event for breast cancer had become an entire nonprofit foundation that has raised more than $1 million to date. The Boarding for Breast Cancer Foundation became something much bigger than ourselves and so it continued. We worked hard and developed traveling educational booths where we taught thousands of young people how to do self breast exams at surfing, skate-boarding, snowboarding, and music events. Our message, Early Detection is the Best Prevention, reached so many people that I sometimes have young women come up to me, not to get an autograph, but to say that because of Boarding for Breast Cancer, they learned how to do a self breast exam and caught a lump. It saved their lives.

They say one person can change the world and I believe that it's true. Individual women were making great strides through snowboarding and other sports and it was obviously having an effect around the world. But I didn't realize the incredible struggles that women in general had made in sports history. Like the first woman to swim the English Channel or the women in the early 1900s who pole-vaulted in hoop skirts. In 2001, Jane Gottesman put together this book called *Gameface* to illustrate through photos and captions what a female athlete looks like, honoring their triumphs and the steps they've made in sports. The book represents female athletes of all kinds throughout the last century. I was honored to have one of my photos selected to be in this book. It was an action shot that photographer Mark Gallup had taken of me jumping on my snowboard off of a cliff up in Canada.

Gameface was premiering as a photo exhibition for the launch of the book at the Smithsonian Institute in Washington, D.C. This museum was something I'd learned about in high school and couldn't believe that my photo would actually be hanging on its walls. My mom and I bought airline tickets right away and flew out for the opening reception. All of these athletes, young and old, were there representing every sport—swimming, baseball, tennis, roller derby...and snowboarding. Being a part of a historical exhibition at the Smithsonian gave me such an incredible feeling of accomplishment. We walked through the gallery looking at all of the photos of the different female athletes and found my photo on the wall. I was so proud of it as I stood next to it to have my picture taken. My mom was blown away by the whole event. She started crying. I don't think she realized what an impact snowboarding had made for women in sports, and now I was being recognized as a part of it all.

At the reception, all of the athletes in the book had stars on their name tags. I was so proud to be wearing a star. I wasn't the token female athlete, but was part of a bigger picture of women in history. I went around to as many athletes as I could to have each of them sign her photo in my book. One girl in particular, Aimee Mullins, really opened my eyes to the challenges women in sports have been through. She was a long jumper and held the record for the 100-meter dash. She opened the book to a picture of her at the Paralympics. I hadn't realized that she had prosthetic legs. It made me think about all of the different struggles that every athlete goes through to accomplish her goals. Every girl in that book, young and old, had all gone through her own pressures and downtimes and had still found that inner strength to rise to the challenge.

One thing I realized is that there are all types of women in sports. Athletes have all different body sizes and shapes. For some sports you need strong arms and strong legs and for others you need balance and grace. It takes coordination in different forms. But the one thing in common across the board is the determination to be your best at something and finding that inner strength. Having the right mind-set and love for your sport gives each female athlete the ability to visualize and be strong enough to achieve her goals.

Being an athlete gave me confidence I never knew I had. That's such an empowering feeling that I continue to hold on to. Sports helped me with my self-esteem throughout my entire life. As for the future of women in sports, I hope that female athletes won't even have to think about being "pretty good for a girl." In my lifetime I hope to see the identity of a female athlete become even stronger and affect everyone. Professional athletes are not the only athletes of the world. If you get up and go jogging every morning, you are a part of this. It's that ambitious and adventurous spirit in all of us that keeps this revolution in motion.

Times have changed just during my years as a snowboarder. Even attitudes have changed. Shannon and I had to wear pink and take a 60-foot jump in Innsbruck to make our mark and show our feminine strength. But I think the best is yet to come. Now, for the first time, women surfers are getting their own signature brands of boards and clothing. Events like the All Girls Skate Jam have started and give girls a chance to compete on an amateur level in skateboarding. With the impact of movies like *Blue Crush* that feature women athletes, girls and women are taking to the ocean. Thanks to some of the pioneering women's sports publications like *W.i.G.*, *Wahine*, and *Fresh and Tasty*, who were showcasing women's action sports before anyone even understood what was going on, it's not unusual to have a woman surfer, skateboarder, or snowboarder on the cover of *Sports Illustrated* or *ESPN* or featured as feminine *and* athletic in *FHM* or *Elle*. Sports aren't just a hobby for women anymore. They are also our way of life.

Snowboarding changed my life. Maybe what happened to me was part of a larger plan—to be there to represent, to show what it means to be a female athlete and push on like that woman at the Boston Marathon

✳ *The Boarding for Breast Cancer booth at the*
Winter X Games in Aspen, Colorado, with
Tara Dakides, Lisa Hudson, Jill Stephens,
and Justine Chiara.

thirty years ago. Maybe it'll bring about another revolution for women twenty years from now.

A few years ago I moved from Utah back to the foothills of Tahoe and bought my own house near my parents. Now, no matter how much I travel for snowboarding, I still feel a comfort returning to northern California where it really feels like home. Sometimes I get scared because my friends are from all over the world and I think, What happens if I stop snowboarding? But I realize that snowboarding has become a permanent part of my life; I won't ever be able to let it go. I'll always be involved in the sport in some way because it's in my heart. In twenty years from now, I'll still be out there, the old lady on the hill, wearing the latest new outfit with my freestyle snowboard under my feet, looking for some powder turns, and loving the life that got me there.

glossary

Ally-oop A trick doing a 180-degree spin in an uphill direction in a halfpipe.

Backcountry Any mountain area that is outside the ski resort.

Backside This can be used to describe a backside air in a halfpipe or doing a backside spin off a jump. If you're goofy, spinning counterclockwise, and if you're regular, spinning clockwise.

Backside wall The wall in the halfpipe that you carve up with your heel-side edge riding forward. If you're looking down at the halfpipe, your backside wall is on your right if you're goofy foot and on your left if you're regular foot.

Big-mountain riding To ride down big mountains with all types of terrain.

Bluebird A clear day without a single cloud in the sky.

Bulletproof Extremely hard snow and ice.

DIY Do It Yourself. A punk expression for making your own clothes, doing your own thing.

Dual Slalom Two racecourses with tight turns set up parallel to each other.

Fakie Riding backward.

Finger chute A narrow path on a big-mountain run that looks like long fingers or spines.

Flat landing To land on a flat slope off of a jump.

Freeriding To ride around the mountain on all types of terrain.

Frontside This can be used to describe a frontside air in the halfpipe or doing a frontside spin off a jump. If you're goofy, spinning clockwise, and if you're regular, spinning counterclockwise.

Frontside wall The wall in the halfpipe that you carve up with your toe-side edge riding forward. If you're looking down at the halfpipe, your frontside wall is on your left if you're goofy foot and on your right if you're regular foot.

Giant Slalom Racecourse with big turns.

Goofy stance When your stance on your board is right foot forward.

Halfpipe A carved-out U-shaped gully in the snow, often man-made with Pipe Dragon snowcats, that you can snowboard on and do tricks in.

Indy air Trick in the air, grabbing your toe-side edge in between your feet with your back hand.

Invert To flip upside down or sideways in a spin or jump.

J-tear A flipping trick that's too hard to explain.

Jam session When a group of friends rides together in the halfpipe or on a jump.

Layback slide Trick in the halfpipe that looks like a layback slash a surfer would do on a wave.

Method air Trick in the air grabbing your heel-side edge in between your feet with your front hand.

Moguls Those damn bumpy things that skiers make on the ski run.

900 Ask Tony Hawk.

Powder The fresh, deep, untracked snow.

Powder line A fresh (meaning no one has skied it) ski run with untracked powder.

Regular stance When your stance on your board is left foot forward.

Rocket air Trick in the air, grabbing the backside edge toward the tip of your snowboard.

Slob air Trick in the air grabbing your toe edge in front of your front foot with your back hand.

Slopestyle An event in competition where there is a series of jumps and rails on one run.

Snowpark A combination of jumps and wooden and metal rails set up at a ski resort for snowboarders and skiers to use as obstacles to slide on or jump over.

Stance The distance between your two bindings, or goofy stance or regular stance.

Superpipe Bigger than a halfpipe—at least 12 feet high from base of the pipe to top of the wall.

competition standings

1986 Soda Springs, 1st Competition   Halfpipe: 3rd

1987 California Series, Donner Ski Ranch   Halfpipe: 1st, Slalom: 1st, Overall: 1st

1987 Shasta, CA   Halfpipe: 1st, Slalom: 1st

1987 World Championships   Halfpipe: 6th

1988 California Series   Overall: 1st

1988 U.S. Time Trials, Purgatory, CO   Slalom: 4th

1988 World Championships   Halfpipe: 6th

1989 U.S. Open, VT   Halfpipe: 4th, Downhill: 7th

1990 USA Halfpipe Champion   1st

1990 World Cup   Halfpipe: 2nd

1990 Pro Tour, Squaw Valley, CA   Halfpipe: 1st, Slalom: 1st

1990 OP Pro Copper Mountain, CO   Halfpipe: 1st

1990 Vuarnet Vertical Air Show   Halfpipe: 1st

1990 California Championships   Halfpipe: 1st, Slalom: 1st

1990 U.S. Open, VT   Halfpipe: 1st

1990 OP Canada, Lake Louise   Moguls: 1st

1990 OP Pro June Mountain, CA   Halfpipe: 1st

1990 OP Canada, Quebec   Slalom: 2nd

1990 U.S. Open   Overall: 2nd

1990 World Cup Colorado   Halfpipe: 2nd

1990 OP Canada, Lake Louise   Halfpipe: 2nd, Giant Slalom: 2nd

1990 Vuarnet Vertical Air Show   Obstacle: 3rd

1990 OP Canada, Quebec   Halfpipe: 3rd

1991 USA Halfpipe Champion   1st

1991 World Cup Overall   Halfpipe: 2nd

1991 OP Pro June Mountain, CA   Halfpipe: 1st, Slalom: 7th

1991 PSTA Mt. Bachelor, OR   Halfpipe: 1st, Giant Slalom: 3rd, Overall: 1st

1991 World Cup Breckenridge   Halfpipe: 2nd

1991 OP Pro Copper Mountain, CO   Halfpipe: 2nd, Giant Slalom: 10th, Slalom: 9th

1991 U.S. Open   Halfpipe: 2nd, Giant Slalom: 15th, Overall: 1st

1991 PSTA Eldora, CO Halfpipe: 2nd, Giant Slalom: 15th

1991 PSTA Arapahoe Basin, CO Halfpipe: 2nd, Giant Slalom: 7th

1991 World Cup Japan Halfpipe: 3rd

1991 PSTA Snow Summit, CA Giant Slalom: 3rd, Halfpipe: 4th, Overall: 1st

1991 Mt. Baker Banked Slalom 5th

1992 USA Halfpipe Champion 1st

1992 TWS Derby Obstacle: 1st

1992 PSTA Snow Summit, CA Halfpipe: 1st

1992 PSTA Squaw Valley, CA Halfpipe: 3rd

1992 OP Pro Copper Mountain, CO Halfpipe: 3rd

1992 PSTA Snowmass, CO Halfpipe: 3rd

1992 World Cup Snowmass, CO Halfpipe: 3rd

1992 World Cup Japan Halfpipe: 3rd

1992 PSTA Big Bear Mountain, CA Halfpipe: 3rd

1992 U.S. Open Halfpipe: 3rd

1992 PSTA June Mountain, CA Halfpipe: 3rd

1993 Westbeach Classic Obstacle: 1st

1993 OP Pro June Mountain, CA Halfpipe: 1st

1993 TWS Derby Big Air: 3rd

1993 World Cup Japan Halfpipe: 3rd

1994 King of the Hill, Valdez, AK Freeride: 2nd

1994 World Cup Europe Halfpipe: 7th

1994 Mt. Hood, OR Halfpipe: 4th

1994 Squaw Valley, CA Halfpipe: 4th

1994 World Cup Japan Halfpipe: 6th

1994 Rocky Mountain Series, Snowmass, CO Halfpipe: 3rd

1994 Mt. St. Anne Canada World Cup Halfpipe: 2nd

1994 U.S. Open Halfpipe: 2nd

1994 World Cup Colorado Halfpipe: 3rd

1994 World Cup Sweden Halfpipe: 2nd

1996 ESPN X Games, Snow Summit Big Air: 3rd, Slopestyle: 4th

1999 MTV Snowed In Big Air: 1st

1998 Airwalk Contest, CO Big Air: 1st

1998 ESPN X Games, Crested Butte, CO Big Air: 1st

1998 ESPN Freeride Contest Big Air: 1st

1998 ESPN Summer X Games Big Air: 2nd

2000 Sims World Championships Big Air: 2nd

Du Pont **SUPPLEX** **U.S. OPEN**

NORTH AMERICAN SNOWBOARD ASSOCIATION

SUPPLEX US OPEN

NASBA RACE CODE No.

MARCH 31, 1990
U.S. SPORTS INC.

STRATTON MOUNTAIN, U.S.A

H A L F P I P E   W O M E N
OFFICIAL RESULTS

TECHNICAL DATA

JURY

TD	TED MARTIN U.S.A	NAME OF THE COURSE (1st/2nd)
REFEREE	ED YROMANS	PIPELINE
ASSISTANT-REF	KEVIN DUNCAN	START
CHIEF OF RACE	SKY FOULKES	FINISH
CHIEF OF COURSE	ANDY MEGROZ	VERTICAL DROP
START REFEREE	A BISCHOFBERGER	HOMOLOG.NO
FINISH REFEREE	DAVID FABRICUS	

HEAD JUDGE: JEFF FULTON

1st RUN

COURSE SETTERS
FORERUNNERS -A-   SETH MORILL   JUDGES: CARTER TURK
        -B-   JAY QUINTIN   MIKE CHANTRY
        -C-   ZACH DIAMOND   KEITH KIMMEL
        -D-

NUMBER OF GATES
START TIME   9:35
WEATHER: FOGGY SNOW: SOFT / ICE TEMPERATURE START: 40   FINISH: 43

	BIB NO	LAST NAME	FIRST	FIRST	SECOND	COMBINED
1	122	BASICH	TINA	106	108	214
2	121	VINCIGUERRA	LISA	110	102	212
3	120	HIGGINS	JEAN	106	102	208
4	133	LOFTHUS	ASHILD	103	100	203
5	148	BORZILLERI	JODY	95	91	186
6	158	RIGGINS	SUZANNE	93	91	184
7	150	DEAN	KATHY	88	89	177
8	137	SMITH	SHANNON	95	78	173
9	127	LEGAZ	KELLY JO	85	83	168
10	123	EBERHARD	TARA	84	82	166
11	160	RIVERA	MEGHAN	86	70	156

🔷 **Stratton**

BURTON
Manchester Center,
Vermont 05255
802 362 4000

APRIL 14, 1990 ---- MOGULS, OFFICIAL FINAL RESULTS, WOME

					HEAD JUDGE:	STEVE EDM
TD:		TED MARTIN		JUDGE:		LEE MARGA
REF:		PAT MCILVAIN		JUDGE:		BOB KLEIN
ASST REF:		NA				
CHF OF RACE:		SHELLY SCHULTZ				
CHF OF CRSE:		DON CAMERON				
START REF:		PAT MCILVAIN				
FIN REF:		TED MARTIN				
TABULATOR:		ANNALISE TOPOROWSKI				
ASSIST TAB:		KAREN MOTT				

WOMEN PLACE	BIB#	NAME	SCORE ROUND 1	SCORE ROUND 2	FINAL COMBINED
			212	188	400
1	25	BASICH, TINA	205	190	395
2	33	TAGGART, MICHELE	193	174	367
3	8	VINCIGUERRA, LISA	169	177	346
4	38	DOLECKI, JENNIFER	149	167	316
	9	BROWN, JULIE			0
		COWRELL, HEATHER	DNS		

			SCORE	SCORE ROUND 2	FINAL COMBINED
					468

DONNER SKI RANCH
SNOWBOARDING CLASSIC
MARCH 13 & 14, 1988
RESULTS, HALFPIPE

MUCH THANKS TO THE FOLLOWING WHO DONATED PRIZES:
AVALANCHE BARFOOT DONNER SKI SHOP FREE FLIGHT GO SKATE
K2 KEMPER OCEAN PACIFIC SKI OPTIKS SKULL SKATE

Judges: Tom Collins, Paula Warberton, Scott Kessler

DIVISION: NOVICE

Plce	BIB#	NAME	1st RUN	2nd RUN	TOTAL
1	122	Andrew Shimer, Homewood	30	22	52
2	268	Greg Navas, Truckee	26	20	46
3	155	Mike Mennick,	18	23	41
4	125	Jake Desrochers, G.Valley	23	17	40
5	265	David Bostick, Roseville	17	18	35
6	262	Ben Hagel, Grass Valley	13	19	32
7	276	Jeff Jacobsen, Stockton	15	14	29
8	260	Tatsunori Morioka, Japan	14	12	26
	156	Jim Stoecker, Portolla Valley	12	14	26
	259	Shigera Ishihara, Japan	12	14	26
	272	Bob Goodsby, Visalia	dns	dns	
	112	Frank Baldridge, 3 Rivers			

DIVISION: WOMEN'S

PLCE	BIB#	NAME	1st RUN	2nd RUN	TOTAL
1	104	Tina Basich, Fair Oaks	28	26	54
2	269	Amy Roberts, Soda Spring	22	20	42
3	111	Karin Jacobson,Tahoe Cty	23	18	41
	108	Kathleen Burke, Truckee	23	18	41
6	274	Bonnie Leary, S.L.T.	22	19	41
7	135	Brinette Battaglia, SLT	17	15	32
8	180	Crystal Aldana, June Lake	13	13	26
9	257	Lexie Hale, Grass Valley	10	12	22
10	270	Stacey Hale, Grass Val.	9		18
	145	Heather Mills, Fair Oaks	DNS		

DIVISION: JR MEN'S

PLCE	BIB#	NAME	1ST RUN	2ND RUN	TOTAL
1	126	Tucker Franson,G.V.	34	35	79
2	147	Chris Roach,Nevada Cty	28	29	57
3	131	Hess Walters,S.L.T.	28	25	53
4	116	Michael Basich, F.O.	27	22	49
5	273	Devin Ryerson, Auburn	24	24	48
6	132	Paul McGill, S.L.T.	24	23	47
	193	Jake Grossi, Carson Cty	21	24	47
8	267	Jon Chance, Portola Val.	27	14	42
9	276	Troy Bellinghausen			41

Donner Ski Ranch, Norden, California

$ *Ticket price:* **$20**   **茶** *Skiable acres:* **435**

☎ **(530) 426-3635**

✈ *Miles from Sacramento Airport:* **90**

This is where it all started for me. The first ski resort in my area to let us snowboarders on the lifts. Owner Norm Sayler was so nice and supportive. He just wanted us kids to have fun and enjoy his mountain. You get the family vibe here and it's a great, inexpensive way to start snowboarding. Norm has kept the prices down on lift tickets and I think you won't find another lift ticket in that price range anywhere. The mountain has a great snowboard park with really fun runs off the back side. I have so many memories at this one. **✳**

Squaw Valley USA, Olympic Valley, California

$ *Ticket price:* **$58**   **茶** *Skiable acres:* **4,000**

☎ **(800) 403-0206**   **@** **www.squaw.com**

✈ *Miles from Reno Tahoe International Airport:* **42**

Squaw still has that lasting impression of being the biggest resort in Tahoe to many snowboarders. There's every kind of terrain here, from big-mountain riding to snowboard parks and multiple halfpipes. It's the true ski town experience with many activities other than snowboarding. **✳**

Snowbird Utah

$ *Ticket price:* **$56**   **茶** *Skiable acres:* **2,500**

☎ **(800) 453-3000**   **@** **www.snowbird.com**

✈ *Miles from Salt Lake City Airport:* **29**

I love Snowbird because of the big-mountain feeling you get riding there. The top of the mountain is accessible by a 125-person tram. This is a great comfort to snowboarders—nothing better than giving your feet a rest out of your bindings for the ride up. Dangling your board off the lift with one leg all day can torque your knee a bit. Utah is also known for its great powder. The light fluffy snow is unique to anywhere else on earth. It's known to have storms that dump up to 5 and 6 feet of snow in a few days. Snowbird is the place to be the day after the storm. The mountain has great terrain features from chutes to cliffs for jumps. There is also a halfpipe for the freestylers of the group. ✳

Wasatch Powder Birds, Utah

$ *Price per day:* **$665–$770**   **❄** *Skiable acres:* **45,000**
☎ **(801) 742-2800**   **@** **www.powderbird.com**

It's always a treat to go helicopter snowboarding in Utah. I always have an amazing day with the Wasatch Powder Bird Guides. The day starts out with a gourmet breakfast and lesson on safety in the backcountry. A complete day is seven runs, which is just enough to satisfy anyone's powder addiction. It might seem effortless to ride the untracked powder in Utah, but here it's enough to wear you out and really test those leg muscles. Extra runs are available if time permits and the sun isn't going down. The terrain has everything from wide-open bowls to cliff-lines for jumping to natural terrain features like huge ridgelines that make a snow wave. To top off the day, Wasatch Powder Bird Guides serve up an excellent dinner and beverage selection. ✳

Out of Bounds Adventures, Haines, Alaska

$ *Price per day:* **$400 to 750**   **❄** *Average vertical feet per day:* **20,000**
☎ **(800) HELL YEA**   **@** **www.alaskaheliskiing.com**

Riding with Out of Bounds Adventures and their guides in Haines, Alaska, is the ultimate backcountry experience. I've had so many adventures here and some of the most scary moments. If you can time it right—weather and snow stability depending—this will be the best heli-snowboarding experience of your life! Make sure your skills are capable and you're warmed up and ready to go. It takes training to be in shape enough to handle such long, hard days of riding huge runs. There are also runs for intermediate riders—it's not all extreme like you see in the movies or on TV. Guides pay attention to your abilities from the beginning so that you won't be in a situation where you cannot get down because it's more than your skills can manage. There is no limit to heli-runs, so start clocking your vertical feet and the race is on! ✳

acknowledgments

To all my girls—Lisa Hudson, I owe my career to you, Gaylene Nagel, Kathleen Gasperini—we did it! Thank you for your patience, Angie Dominguez, Sherryl Lynn, Keri Jones, Shannon Dunn, Barrett Christy, Leslee Olson, Michele Taggart, Megan Pischki, Janna Meyen, Tara Dakides, Leah Butler, Tami Bradley, Erica Bartfield, Tiffany Aldrich, Laura Schwan, Kristen Berry, Christine Chung, Kayte Peck Guerrero, Moniqua Plante, Sarah Haynes, Melanie Morano, Shelbee Meed, April Todd, Catalin Kaiser, Emily Sullivan, Heather Mills, Natalie Murphy, Darryl Hannah, Justine Chiara, Lyndsey Roach, Jamie McCloud, Jen Hannet, Jerry Mahathy, Laurie Bula, Debbie Monroe, Kim Peterson, Pettit Guilwee, Lisa Klien, Trish Burns, Clair Jonson, Shantie, Kelly Wright, Victoria Jealouse, Karen Lewandowski, Abby Guyer, Circe Wallace, Morgan LaFonte, Stacy Tricky, Megan Griffith, Jessica Ballard, Marchella Churchhill, Mona, Kayo Ishibe, Dana, Kennedy, Lovie, Shelly, Jessica Dalpiaz, Jean Higgins, Kelly-Jo Legaz, Lisa Vensigerra, Amy Howett, Tara Eberhardt, Betsy Shaw, Shelly Walsh.

To my family for all of their love and support.—my parents, Michael, Skip and Joy Pisor, Tony and Pattie and Jackie Free, Chrissy and Oren and Brittney, Gramps, Grandma Mary, Grampa Bruggman, Grandma Dorothy, Grandpa Harry, Aunt Marqie, Uncle Don and Aunt Eva, Uncle Dickie and Aunt Larrie, the Routts, Aunt Jude and Elaine, Sid and Dianne Turner, the Adams, Auntie Annie, Uncle Steve, Uncle Tom.

To my extended family and friends—the Poers, the Percys, the Todds, the McCrarys, the Kaisers, the Sullivans, Robin Dalley, Inga Krauss, Robin Primavera and Alee, Montie and Boys, the LaCosts, the Hornors, the Cottrells, Tuffer and Stacy Patrick, Gene Burns, Eric Long, Mikki and Ken.

To all of my Sac friends—the memories are forever—Bucky Helwick, Heather and Stuart Jansma, Blue and Sophia, Holland and Cindy Hollingsworth, Don and Danielle Bostic, Charlie Adams, Larry "Slo" Peterson, Randy Smith, Ricky Windsor, Scott Mugford, Troy Clower, Eric Silva, Brenden and Tristen, Nathan Carrico, Mark Hornor, Sheila and Jordie, Brian and Shelly, Punker Bill, Mitch Weathers, Steve-O, Kevin Costa, Sam Cunningham, Chris and Andy Olivera, Scott Lowmirer, Casey, Jon Brockway, Matt, Eden King, Kurt Harvill, Snaggle, Jerry Johnson, Ross Goodman.

To all of my friends who helped my career with photographs, filming, and magazine coverage—thank you for your encouragement, your photos tell my story—Justin Hostynek, Trevor Graves, Alibaba, Eithan Fotier, Bill Gallen, Jon Shapiro, Richard Cheski, Scott Soens, Mark Gallup, Jeff Curtis, Nate Christensen, John Kelly, Whitey, Andy Wright, Scott Sullivan, Chris Carnel, Jon Foster, Kevin Zacher, Ruben Sanchez, Stan Evans, Eric Burger, Shem Roose, Jess Gibson, Ian Ruter, Chris Owens, Tamera Davis, Dave Simmers, Ben Meyren, Al, Chris Zam, Scott Mellini, Jimmy Lu, Mike McEntire, *Snowboarder Magazine* crew, *Transworld Snowboarding* magazine crew, Kanomi, Infograms, Pat Bridges, Doug Palladini, Scott Sullivan, Ross Stephy, Pattie Sagovie, Brice Knights.

To all of my team managers, sponsors, teachers, teammates, and friends in the industry for their inspiration and unbelievable support through the years— much love—Paul Gomez, Paul Frank, Chris Stiepock, Terry Harty, Morgan Stone, Shon Tomlin, Pat Parnell, Austin Brown, Mark Rieter, Ian Voterri, Mike Artz, Travis Wood— thanks for always being there for me, GT, Chad DiNenna, Andy Latts, Cory Smith, Jake Burton, Jon Textor, Tom Sims, Jamie Salters, Dave Kemper, Alistair Craft, Troy and Trent Bush, Joel Gomez, John Silva, Dave Ray, Ken Block, Mark Hibton, Steve Ruff, Peter Line, Montel, Chris Sayda, Eric Kotch, Brad Steward, Scott Rouse, Fran Richards, Carl Harris, Lisa and John Logic, Jack Rebbetoy, Kurt Zach, Joe Babcock, Mr. Hase, Church Churchhill, Tom Shoenhair, Sal Masekela, Mrs. Aldamam, Mr. Wakfodrevans, Ian Klienert, Josh Behar, Robert Earl—this book happened because of you!—Devun Walsh, Dionne Delesalle, Allan Clark, Todd Fransen, Adam Mariman, Jamie Lynn, Jonny Moseley, Andy Hetzel, Dave Lee, Jesse Fulton, Josh Derksen, Billy and Jeff Anderson, Matty and Kathy Goodman, Dave Dowd, Brad Makepeace, Tim Windell, Craig Kelly, Terje Hakkonsen, Jeremy and Tiff Jones, Kareem Cambell, Dave Downing, Dan Schipper, Todd and Lindsey Richards, Mike Lucas, Evan Banard, Dave Grohl, Nate Mendle, Taylor Hakins, Noah Salasnek, Aaron Vincent, Chris Stepock, Brian Dorfman, Tom Nashida, Chris Burke, Roger, Lee Crane.

Special thanks to all my sponsors who have supported me over the years— GoSkate, Sims, Airwalk, Op, Smith, Fishpaw, Swag, Prom, Tuesday, Hurley, Nixon, Ally, Paul Frank, 241, Zumiez.

To my friends in Utah who know the true meaning of a bluebird powder day after a storm—Keri and Scott Biesinger, Cody Dresser, Blue Montgomery, Marc Frank, Kurt Wastell, Brian Botts, Kate and Amy, Bennie, Ox, Dan and Sara, Celia, Maria, Drew, Dennis, George, Brian, Thien, Travis Parker, Bobby Meeks, Jason Bump, Adam Yauch, Kevin and Oli and the boys at Wasatch Powder Bird.

To Sean Dog and Bruce Griggs for your guidance in Alaska.

To the Donner crew—where it all started—Norm Sayler, Damian Sanders, the

Nicholsen family, Jim and Bonnie Zellers, Tom Burt, Terry Kidwell, Jimbo Morgan, Shaun Palmer, Jeff Grail, Chris and Monty Roach, Dave Seoane, the Fransen family, Tom Collins, Scooter, Mike Jacoby, Kyle, Shawn Goulart, Heath, Devin Ryerson, Jon Biocchi, Willie, Amy Rogers, Mike Chanchry, Dave Weaver, Chris Carnel, Bud Fawcett, Lori Dominguez, Tim McCrary.

To all of my friends that make my hometown so special—Stuart Shapes, Jeanne and Bo, Sharon and Stephano, Bruce and Caroline, Sheri Barley, Bob and Peggy Wright, Jim and Jane Moran, Vikki and Al, Layne Williams, Matt and Kelly Alsop, the Heitsberg family, Patrick Czarnowski, Jay Sydman—your generosity will never be forgotten, Kelly and Rich, Bram, the Lacoste family, Daniella and Knell, Kathren and David, Gelasio, David Vertin, Chris Owens, Melody, Stan and Donna Levin, Susanne and Ru, Robear, Michael and Patti, Jo, George, John and Irean, Jean, Perry and Miu, Jim Warner.

To Brian Dorfman and Stephen Tamaribuchi and Perry for your healing powers.

To Mel Hurt—file an extension for my taxes, it's snowing in Utah!

To Cory Cottrell for your love and support.

A special thanks to everyone who has supported Boarding for Breast Cancer over the years—we are making a difference!

Sorry if I forgot anyone—it's 3 A.M. and the book is due tomorrow!

—TINA BASICH

I'd like to sincerely thank Thomas Scott Wallace for providing the love and support I needed to write freely on this book, and to my mother, Alice Campbell Gasperini, for showing me the many layers of beauty and strength that women truly represent.

—KATHLEEN GASPERINI